THE RELIGIOUS ATTITUDES
OF THE INDO-EUROPEANS

ISBN: 0-906879-51-5

Reprinted June 2001

Historical Review Press
PO Box 62,
Uckfield, Sussex,
TN22 1ZY,
United Kingdom.

North American Distributor:
A. B. C. Books
P.O. Box 212
Decatur, Il 62525
U. S. A.

The
RELIGIOUS ATTITUDES
of the
INDO-EUROPEANS

translated from the German of

PROFESSOR HANS FK GÜNTER

by

Vivian Bird
in collaboration with
Roger Pearson M.SC. (Econ).

Historical Review Press
England

"The nobly born must nobly meet his fate."
Euripides

"Courage leads to heaven, fear to death."
Seneca

"There they stood... the immortals who are
the source of all our blessings
Homer: Odyssey

CONTENTS

FOREWORD
TO THE SIXTH GERMAN EDITION

I HOPE that the re-appearance of this work after almost thirty years may help the younger generation to give more attention to the religious history of the whole of the Indo-European area, in contrast to previous generations, for a better knowledge of the Indo-European world will lead the West (to which North America belongs) towards self-realisation. Heraclitus, as Aristotle reported (*Concerning the parts of Animals* I, 5 :645) instructed strangers visiting him, who hesitated on his threshold, to draw closer to him with the words: "Enter, for here the Gods also dwell!" May this work, in its present edition, express a similar invitation.

If, in our era of the "Decline of the West", the last remnants of the Western Indo-European peoples are submerged due to the dearth of true-blooded Nordics, then nevertheless the last few survivors will retain that same Indo-European conviction which supported and inspired "the last Romans" (*Romanorum ultimi*) who witnessed the conversion of the aristocratic Roman republic into the "de-Romanised" empire — the proud belief in inflexible and unyielding courage before destiny which will be portrayed in this work as characteristically Indo-European, and above all Nordic — an ideal which Horace also described in the words:

Quocirca vivite fortes,
Fortiaque adversis opponite pectora rebus!

(Sermones, 2, 135/36)

Hans F. K. Günther
Bad Heilbrunn
Early Spring 1963

CHAPTER ONE

Freedom is where you can live, as pleases a brave heart; where you can live according to the customs and laws of your fathers; where you are made happy by that which made your most distant ancestors happy.

E M Arndt, *Catechism for the Teutonic Soldier and Warrior*, 1813.

IN this work I want to advance some reflections on the religiosity of the Indo-Europeans — that is to say, the Indo-European speaking peoples originating from a common Bronze Age nucleus — who have always exerted a significant influence on the government and spirit of predominantly Nordic races[1]. Just as by comparing the structure of the Indian, Persian, Sacaean, Armenian, Slavic and Baltic languages, and of the Greek, Italian, Celtic and Teutonic dialects, we can reach a conclusion as to a common or primal Indo-European language, approximating to the latter part of the early Stone Age, in the same way, an examination of the laws and legal customs of the different peoples of Indo-European language reveals a primal Indo-European feeling for law.[2] Similarly, from a comparison of the religious forms of these peoples we can identify a particular religious attitude emanating from the Indo-European nature – a distinctive behaviour of Indo-European men and people towards the divine powers.

So it is that certain common religious attitudes, which originally were peculiar to all peoples of Indo-European language, reveal the identity of an Indo-European religiosity. But since in fact all Indo-European nations represented different types moulded on the spiritual pattern of the Nordic race, the origin of these common religious attitudes may be identified in a religiosity which is characteristically Nordic, emanating from the spiritual nature of the Nordic race.[3]

It is fortunate that for our knowledge of this Nordic religiosity, we do not have to rely solely upon Teutonic religious forms,[4] for the information we possess about the Teutonic forms of belief is regrettably inadequate. It is all the more incomplete as it is derived from a late period in the development of these forms, which had already been influenced by religious ideas from Hither-Asia, from the Mediterranean basin and from the Celtic west of Europe, where the Druids had begun to distort the ancient Indo-European religiosity of the Celts so that they no longer bore a purely Nordic stamp. The Teutonic Gods, the Aesirs (cf. Oslo, Osnabruck, in High German: Ansen, cf. Anshelm, Ansbach), had already absorbed the Vanir who had spread from south-east Europe (F R Schroeder: *Germanentum und Alteuropa*, Germanisch-Romanische Monatsschrift XXII, 1934, p187) without thoroughly reinterpreting them in a purely Teutonic spirit. Likewise, from south-east Europe and Hither-Asia, the God Dionysos had been accepted among the Olympian Gods without being fully re-interpreted, even being found in Homer, and only later becoming a native blond God instead of an alien, dark-haired one. The pre-Christian Teutons have with justice been compared with the Achaeans, who were their nearest relatives, and it can be shown that much that the Hellenes incorporated into their belief and religiosity in post-Homeric times was more or less alien to the Indo-European spirit, as for example the Orphic mysteries. Thus late on in their period of pagan development the Teutons had accepted much that was contradictory to the Indo-European nature. What non-Indo-European or non-Teutonic characteristics have been imparted to the Teutonic God Odin (Wodan, Wuotan)? Odin, with his strange blend of "loftiness and deception",[5] is undoubtedly no longer the ideal example of an Indo-European or Teutonic God, and his worship is no longer characteristic of the Indo-European or the original Teutonic religion. Already one perceives in him the voice of an alien, non-Nordic race.

One must ask how much of Odin's character can be explained from Teutonic folk belief, how much is later poetical embellishment, and how much reaches back, as with Zeus or Jupiter, into antiquity and the Indo-European conception of the "Father of the Heavens". We must not overlook the fact, stressed by Andreas Heusler in *Germanentum* (1934, pp. 95-106 and cf. also Erik Therman: *Eddan och dess Ödestragik*, 1938, pp. 65, 105, io6) that "the Edda mythology is largely a Norwegian-Icelandic poetical creation of the Viking era", elaborated by the poets who dwelt at the courts of local Norwegian princes during the late pagan and early Christian era, at a time when many Teutons were uprooted from their native soil and exposed to alien ideas. According to Hensler, Odin is a "new creation of Teutonic religious phantasy", and above all, a God of war and of the Viking princes, warriors and skalds. However, as a war God, Odin is an incalculable force to reckon with, "capable of deceit", as L M Derolez informs us (*De Godsdienst der Germanen*, 1959, p. 79).

The worship of Odin (Wotan or Wuotan in the High German form) spread from west Scandinavia during the warlike Folk Wandering and Viking era to the Vandals and Langobards, and to the Saxons in Lower-Saxony and in England, but it always predominantly appealed to the local princes and their retinue and to the skalds of the princes' courts, to whom the war God was also the God of poetry. Perhaps it is the name which is the unique feature of Odin that reaches back into Indo-European antiquity, for its root is derived from the Indo-European word *vat* meaning "to be spiritually excited", and as such it is still preserved in Sanskrit, in old Iranian and in Latin, where it corresponds to the word *vates*, meaning a seer or a poet.

The concept of Odin-Wodan appears at its highest form in the grandiose *Edda* mythology of the twilight of the Gods, the end of the world, Ragnarök, but it is an expression more of poetry than belief. The yeoman freeholders on their hereditary farms, who formed the majority of the Teutonic peoples, were never at ease with the cult of Odin or Wodan (Karl Helm: *Wodan; Ausbreitung und Wanderung seines Kults*, Giessener Beitrige zur deutschen

Philologie, Vol. LXXXV, 1946; RLM Derolez: *De Godsdienst der Germanen*, 1959, p79 *et seq*). According to Erik Therman (*op. cit.*, pp. 23, 77, 106), many sagas of the Gods of the *Edda* and also of Odin do not belong to the folk belief of the Teutons, but instead are an expression of the ideals and concepts of the Viking nobility and of the local North Teutonic princes.

One must above all bear in mind, when dealing with the figure of Odin, what Jan de Vries has written in *The Present Position of Teutonic Religious Research* (Germanische Monatsschrift, Vol. XXIII, 1951, p1 *et seq*.): "Proceeding solely from the sources of Teutonic religious history, research will never arrive at conclusive results concerning the nature of Teutonic religion: for illumination of Teutonic belief and religious attitudes, it will be necessary to return again and again to Indo-European religion and mythology".

Georges Dumezil has also expressed the same warning.

The figure of Odin-Wodan does not belong to Indo-European religious history. He is the special God of the loosely-rooted expanding Viking Folk, and his composite personality stems from the late period of Teutonic paganism, and as such does not help to throw light on Indo-European religious attitudes.

Again, in one's search for material to clarify this religiosity, there is little of value to be found in the descriptions of the religions of the Celts and the Slavs. Throughout the broad areas under their rule — and the Galatians penetrated as far as Asia Minor — the Celts formed only a thin upper layer holding sway over pre-Indo-European peoples governed by matriarchal family systems, whose linguistic forms deeply influenced the Celtic dialects, and whose spiritual beliefs transformed the original religious attitudes of the Celts.

The religious customs and moral attitudes of matriarchal origin emanating from the lower, non-Celtic strata, which penetrated the religion of the Celts, (Wolfgang Krause: *Die Kelten, Religionsgeschichtliches Lesebuch*, Vol. XXIII, 1929), have been compared by both Marie Sjöstedt, in *Dieux et Heroes des Celtes*, (1940, p126) and by Jan de Vries, in *Keltische Religion* (1961, p224), with those of primitive non-European tribes, and from the Indo-European point of view, the latter must be described as repellent.

Finally, the hierarchy of the Celtic Druids, a powerseeking priestly order, was non-Indo-European in character, and resembled in structure the recent Brahmin system of caste-rule in India.

The records of the pre-Christian religions of Slavic tribes (A Brückner: *The Slavs*, in *Religionsgeschichtliches Lesebuch*, Vol. III, 1926, and Karl H Meyer: *Die Slavische Religion*, in Carl Clemen's *Die Religionen der Erde*, 1927 pp 237 *et seq.*), handed down to us by the Christian historians of the sixth century, Procopius and Jordanes, have been distorted by mistaken interpretation, or by writers who were hostile to the pagan Slavs, and they have little material of any value to offer. Arabic and Teutonic records are equally deficient, but something may be deduced from the morals and customs, and the sagas and songs which have been preserved and re-interpreted by Christianity. From them we receive an impression that the early Indo-Europeans worshipped their ancestors and believed that the houses they inhabited and the lands and animals that belonged to them were possessed of guardian spirits, features that were characteristic of early Latin beliefs.

Fortunately, however, the religious forms of the other Indo-European speaking peoples bear many details which guide us back to a more profound study of primary Indo-European religiosity, and in the beliefs of the early Indians, the early Persian[6] and the early Hellenes, one can, in my opinion, trace essentially Indo-European elements and the basic factors vital to grasping and understanding them. Only by comparing all these forms of belief — and those of the Italici must not be omitted — with the Teutons' can we obtain a clearer picture of Nordic-Teutonic religiosity.

If I thus attempt to express here in words individual features of this picture, I do so in an endeavour to ascertain, subject to the limitations of my own knowledge (for I am not a scholar of religious science) not only what is primary in all the religious forms of Indo-European speaking peoples known to us, but also what is their purest and richest unfolding. My concern is not with any search for the so-called primitive in these religious forms, nor whether this or that higher idea is deduced from some lower stage of old Stone-Age magical belief or middle Stone-Age spirit belief (animism). I am solely interested in determining the pinnacles of Indo-European religion. My concern is to identify Indo-European religion at its most perfect and characteristic form, and in its richest and purest assertion — that completely spontaneous expression of the spirit in which primary Indo-European nature expresses itself with the greatest degree of purity.

But when I speak of the richest unfolding of religious forms, I do not mean those eras characterised by a confusing multitude of ideas, which sometimes intrude upon the Indo-European peoples, for at these periods the primal Nordic has become permeated with ideas alien to his nature. On the contrary, I believe that Indo-European religious life had already attained heights of great richness amongst the individual Indo-European tribes in the Bronze Age, so that the Bronze Age Nordic experienced much of the flowering of the religiosity of his race. Each time this religiosity unfolded it flourished for a succession of centuries, indeed often up to a millenia, until a spirit alien in nature — and usually corresponding to a general weakening of the Nordic racial strain — permeated the original religious ideas of the Indo-Europeans, and then expressed in their language religious ideas which were no longer purely or even predominantly European.

My aim, therefore, is to comprehend Indo-European religion in its richest and purest unfolding. It can be traced, for example, in Hellenic poetry from Homer to Pindar and Aeschylus — though strictly speaking, perhaps only up to Pindar, or, in more general terms, up to the fifth century before our time of reckoning[7] — and later, with Sophocles and Plato, who looked back in many aspects, Indo-European religiosity again predominates, but now as the religiosity of individual men and not of an entire circle of their aristocracy.

I shall confine myself to describing primary or essential attitudes of the Indo-Europeans, omitting all that they have expressed in their various languages, in their arts, and in the customs of their daily life in the early and middle periods of their development; for were one to include in a description of Indo-European religious

attitudes every form to which they have given expression throughout their history, one would find features amongst them of nearly
every religion. It would be easy, therefore, to quote examples
of those forms of religion which I describe below as non-Indo-
European, from the religious life of Indo-European peoples, especially
in later times, or, in ethnological terms, in the de-Nordicised
period. Indeed, people have even spoken in an erroneous way of a
"Christian antiquity".' What I described as Indo-European religiosity thus pertains to those periods in the history of the Indo-
European peoples when the soul of the Nordic race could still
express itself with sufficient vigour.

However, I do not overlook the fact that in many instances the
rich and pure unfolding of Indo-European religiosity was preserved
and carried forward into later periods. Examples of this, which I
will consider later, are the noble art of the Panathenaea festival
procession on the frieze in the Parthenon of the Acropolis of Athens (Maxime Collignon: *Le Parthenon*, Vol. III, 1912, Table 78 *et
seq.*; Ernst Langlotz: *Phidias Probleme*, 1947, p27 *et seq.*; and his
Schönheit und Hoheit, 1948; Reinhard Lullies: *Griechische Plastik*, 1956,
p22, Table 147 *et seq.*;) or the noble art of the ara pacis Augustae —
the altar of peace dedicated in the year 9 B.C. under Octavianus
Augustus in Rome (Giuseppe Moretti: *Die Ara Pacis Augustae*, 1948;
Robert Heidenreich, Die Bilder der ara pacis Augustae, Neue
Jahrbücher für Antike und Deutsche Bildung, 1 Year 1938, p31 *et
seq.*) — and likewise the carmen sacculare of the Roman poet Horace
(Horatius, *Carmina* 111, 25.)

I would not regard as Indo-European every religious idea which
has been found amongst individual Indo-European speaking
peoples, but many of them were divided into racial strata in such a
way that the rulers were predominantly men of Nordic race. Therefore, probably much of the preoccupation with magic and the
haunting of the spirit which is described to us as Indo-European
religious thought is in reality an expression of the religiosity of the
lower racial stratas, the non-Nordic linguistically Indo-
Europeanised subject people. Different peoples are often said to
have a lower mythology in contrast to the higher mythology of the

same people, and it is often the case that the lower mythology had no relation whatever with the higher, and that the lower stratum of the people found expression in one mythology and the leading stratum in another. Where Indo-European society consists in such racial layers of predominantly Nordic farmers, aristocracy and patriarchs, superimposed on non-Nordic peoples, Indo-European religiosity can only be sought in the religious ideas of the upper strata. This is also proved by the fact that Indo-European religiosity is always directly linked with the conviction of the value of birth and pride in heredity, and that man has an unalterable hereditary nature and an inborn nobility which it is his duty to society to maintain — as is particularly apparent, for example, in the truly Hellenic religiosity of Pindar.[9]

It is thus important to realise, when studying the religious history of all Indo-European speaking peoples, that the upper stratum represented more closely the traditional ideas of belief. Therefore, for example, Carl Clemen's chapter on the ancient Indo-European Religion in his *Religionsgeschichte Europas* (Vol. 1, 1926, pp162 *et seq.*) makes almost no contribution to our knowledge of Indo-European religiosity. One cannot assume uncritically that all the pre-historic and historic information collected from all the regions where the Indo-European tongue was spoken constitutes evidence of roughly equivalent value. More than half of what Clemen cites as Indo-European religious thought, I regard as the ideas of the underlayer of Indo-Europeanised peoples of non-Nordic race. Similarly, the descriptions of the Hellenic world of belief by the outstanding Swedish scholar, P Nilson, in his *Griechischer Glaube* (1950), contains much which originates from the non-Nordic sub-strata, and does not correspond to the form of belief and religiosity of the ancient Hellenes of early Stone Age and Bronze Age central Europe. The same observation holds true for the majority of the descriptions of the religious world of Rome.

On the other hand, much which has asserted itself in Islamic Persia and in Christian Europe in religious life can be valued as a resurgence of Nordic Indo-European religiosity, as would be expected, for inherited nature will always stir against alien forms of belief. Thus the mysticism of the Islamised Persians, Sufism, is to be understood as a breakthrough by Indo-European religiosity into an alien and compulsive faith, as an expression of the disposition of the race-soul or "racial endowment" as described by RA Nicholson.[10] A large part of the mysticism of the Christianised West may also be regarded as a similar breakthrough. Among great church leaders of both Christian faiths, religiosity of Indo-European kind is expressed whenever they allow the innermost essence of their religiosity to assert itself within them completely undogmatically. I would also be able to describe many a feature of Indo-European religiosity in the words of recent German poets. Examples of Indo-European religiosity can be found in Shakespeare, Winckelmann, Goethe, Schiller, Hölderlin, in Shelley and Keats, in Hebbel, Gottfried Keller and Storm, and there are many others in the literature, philosophy and plastic arts of the western peoples.[11]

In his work *Der Glaube der Nordmark* (1936), which has passed through many editions, and which has also been translated into Danish and Swedish, Gustav Frenssen described the religiosity of the country people he knew in North Germany, having gained a deep insight into their minds and hearts as their pastor. Without it being the intention of the author, the work became a description of Indo-European religion in the rural environment of a North German people. H. A. Korff, in his *Faustischer Glaube* (1938) has attempted to describe the belief to which Goethe confessed in his poem *Faust*:

> "It is belief in life in spite of all: in spite of the knowledge of
> the fundamentally tragic character of life." (op. cit., 1938, p155)

Such a belief in life is characteristic of Indo-European religion.

In his work *Weltfrömmigkeit* (1941), Eduard Spranger has described the sublime religiosity of the great men in German spiritual life at the end of the eighteenth and the beginning of the nineteenth century — a fundamentally Indo-European religiosity which Spranger, however, sought to link with a Christianity wrested from the dogmas of the Church. He noticed that religious motives resounded through great German poetry and German idealistic philosophy, but deceived himself, overlooking the increasing desolation of spiritual life in Europe and North America, into assuming that these motives still mean a great deal to present day Germans, Europeans and North Americans. In North America, Ralph Waldo Emerson (1803-1882)was one of the last writers to reveal a strong Indo-European religiosity.

A scientific analysis of the Indo-European nature in religious life, similar to Walter F Otto's analysis of Hellenic religiosity[12] has still — as far as I am aware — to be accomplished. There are good and there are mediocre descriptions of the forms of belief of individual Indo-European speaking peoples. But there is no satisfactory exposition of Indo-European religiosity as such, and where such a description has been attempted, it is often either deliberately or unconsciously measured with yard-sticks derived from the Jewish-Christian world. We owe it to ourselves, however, as Teutons and as Indo-Europeans to seek out the true nature of Indo-European religiosity.

It would be presumptuous on my part to imagine that my observations constitute a decisive foundation for research into this subject. More than suggestions I cannot promise. But I shall indicate in what fields I hope it might be possible to find assertions of Indo-European religiosity in both its rich and pure form, and also where this is not possible. I will merely explain what I have observed in relation to questions which have occupied me from my youth onwards, and how I have done so. This work is therefore in the nature of an outline of the impressions influencing me, arising from my interest over many years in the Indo-European world.

CHAPTER TWO

L ET US take several examples of ways in which IndoEuropean religiosity did not assert itself, so as to recognise later how in fact it did express itself with the greatest purity and freedom. I shall attempt, wherever possible, to look away from the religion of the individual Indo-European peoples and to describe only the common characteristic feelings with which the Indo-Europeans face the divine, no matter in what shape they imagine this divinity. If it must be described with words, then I would say: not the religion, nor the religions, but the religiosity of the Indo-Europeans is what I attempt to distinguish.

In the first place, it is unmistakeably evident that Indo-European religiosity is not rooted in any kind of fear, neither in fear of the deity nor in fear of death. The words of the latter-day Roman poet, that fear first created the Gods (Statius, *Thebais*, III, 661: *primus in orbe fecit deos timor*), cannot be applied to the true forms of Indo-European religiosity, for wherever it has unfolded freely, the "fear of the Lord" (Proverbs, Solomon ix. 10; Psalm 111, 30) has proved neither the beginning of belief nor of wisdom.

Fear could not arise because the Indo-European does not consider that he is the creature of a deity; he neither regarded himself as a "creature" nor did he comprehend the world as a creation – the work of a creative God with a beginning in time. To him the world was far more a timeless order, within which both Gods as well as men had their time, their place and their office. The idea of creation is Oriental, above all Babylonic, like the idea — coming from Iran, but not from the Indo-Aryan spirit — of the world's end, culminating in a judgment and the intercession of a kingdom

19

of God, in which everything will be completely transformed.

After the ageing Plato had taken over, in *Timaios*, certain features of the oriental theory of creation, legends for the explanation of the origin of the world, his pupil Aristotle (*Concerning the Heavens*, edited by Paul Cohlke, 1958, pp26-27) re-established the Indo-European outlook: the world totality is "without becoming, it is intransitory, eternal, without alteration, without growth or diminution".

The Indo-Europeans believed — revealing a premonition of the knowledge and hypotheses of physics and astronomy of our present day — in a succession without end or beginning, of world origins and world endings, in repeated twilights of the Gods and in renewals of the world and of the Gods in a grandiose display, exactly as is described in the *Völuspa* of the *Edda*. They believed in repeated cataclysms, such as the Hellenes described, upon which new worlds with new Gods would follow.[13] A succession of world creations and world endings was taught by Anaximandros, Heraclitus, Empedodes and other Hellenic thinkers, and later by the Roman poet and thinker Lucretius. The latter (*de rerum natura*, V. 95 *et seq.*) expected the world to end in this fashion:

> And yet a single day suffices to o'erthrow
> A thousand ages built, this world we know.

According to Andreas Heusler (*Germanentum*, 1934, pp 95, 106 *et seq*) "destruction of existence was a firm expectancy for the Teutons, renewal of life an uncertain premonition". As Erik Therman said (*op cit*, pp. 64, 213), to them the world was a destiny — a super-powerful causal connection.

The belief in the end, the eschatology of the East Iranian Spitama Zarathustra, which was linked with the belief in a coming world saviour, has been described by HS Nyberg (*Die Religionen des Atten Orients, Mitteilungen der Vorderasiatisch-Ägyptischen Gesellschaft* 34. Vol. I, 1938, pp 266 *et seq.*, 231 *et seq.*). It subsequently penetrated into Judaism shortly before the time of Jesus and fully determined his message (Heinrich Ackermann: *Jesus, Seine Botschatt und deren Aufnahme, im Abendland*, 1952, pp42 *et seq*; *ibid, Entstellung und*

Klärung der Botschaft Jesu, 1961, pp225 *et seq*).

In Iran, the influence of Hither Asiatic beliefs had resulted in the idea of the repeated rise and fall being converted into a belief in the approaching end of the world, an end of the world which a saviour (*saoshyant*) will precede and upon which judgment of the world will follow. Yet despite this, Indo-European thought revived to the extent that the Iranians did not conceive of the world as a creation, nor of God as a creator, and thus the feeling of being a creature being enchained by the will of the creator could not find expression.

Still less was a religious attitude possible here, which saw in man a slave under an all-powerful Lord God. The submissive and slavish relation of man to God is especially characteristic of the religiosity of the Semitic peoples. The names Baal, Moloch, Rabbat and others, all stress the omnipotence of the Lord God over enslaved men, his creatures, who crawl on their faces before him. For the Indo-Europeans the worship of God meant the adoration of a deity, the encouragement and cultivation of all impulses to worship, it meant *colere*, with the Romans and *therapeuein* with the Hellenes. In the Semitic language the word worship comes from its root abad, which means to be a slave. Hanna (I Samuel i. 11) begs Jahve, the Hebrew tribal God, to give her, his slave, a son. David (2 Samuel vii. 18) calls himself a slave of his God, and so does Solomon (2 Kings iii. 6). The essence of Jahve is terror (2 Moses xxiii. 27; Josiah viii. 13), but this has never been true of the Indo-Europeans' Gods. The Hymns to Zeus of the stoic Kleanthes of Assos (331-233 — Max Pohlenz: *Die Stoa*, 1948, pp 108 *et seq.*, and G. Verbeke: *Kleanthos van Assos, Verhandelingen van den koninklijke Academie vor Wetenschapen, Letteren en Schone Kunsten van Belgic, Klasse der Letteren*, Year XI, Nr. 9, 1949, p235), from which Paul (Apostles xvii. 28) took words to adjust himself to the Hellenic religious outlook, completely contradicts for example, the religiosity of the 90th Psalm.

In Christianity the conduct of the faithful before God is freely interpreted by the term *humilis*, and hence humility, meaning literally slave mind or serving the tribe, is demanded as the essence of religiosity. But this is non-Indo-European in outlook, an after-effect of oriental religiosity. Because he is not a slave before an omnipotent God, the Indo-European mostly prays not kneeling nor prostrated to earth, but standing with his eyes gazing upward and his arms stretched out before him.

As a complete man with his honour unsullied, the honest Indo-European stands upright before his God or Gods. No religiosity which takes something away from man, to make him appear smaller before a deity who has become all-powerful and oppressive, is Indo-European. No religiosity which declares the world and man to be valueless, low and unclean, and which wishes to redeem man to overearthly or superhuman sacred values, is truly Indo-European. Where "this world" is dropped, and in its place the "other world" is raised to eternal good, there the realm of Indo-European religiosity is abandoned. For Indo-European religiosity is of this world, and this fact determines its essential forms of expression. As a result it is sometimes difficult for us to comprehend its greatness today, because we are accustomed to measuring religiosity in terms of values taken from decidedly non-Indo-European and mainly oriental religious life, and especially from mediaeval and early modern Christianity. It follows therefore that our view of Indo-European religiosity must suffer in the same way as would one's view of the structure of the Indo-European languages if they were described in terms of characteristics appropriate to the Semite languages. We are today accustomed to seek true religiosity only in terms of the other world and to regard religiosity of this world as undeveloped or lacking in some aspect — a preliminary stage on the way to something more valuable. Thus the Jewish-Christian religious ideas transmitted to us prevent us from recognisirig the greatness of the Indo-European religiosity, so that in comparative religious studies Indo-European religious values are again and again represented purely scientifically as being less important, since the proponents of these views have unconsciously accepted the ideal of Oriental spiritual values as a yardstick for every religious value. This criticism is also applicable to Rudolf Otto's study called *The Sacred* (1948). Thus the greatness and fullness of the Indo-

European world is never recognised.

Whoever wishes to measure religiosity by the degree of man's abasement before the divine, or by how questionable, valueless or even tainted "this world" appears to man when faced with that "other world", and whoever wishes to measure religiosity by the degree to which man feels a cleft between a transitory body and an indestructible soul, between flesh (*sarx*) and spirit (*pneuma*) — whosoever seeks to do this will have to declare that the religiosity of the Indo-Europeans is truly impoverished and paltry.

Gods and men are not, in the eyes of the Indo-Europeans, incomparable beings remote from one another, least of all to the Hellenes, to whom Gods appeared as immortal men with great souls (cf. Aristotle: *Metaphysics*, 111, 2,997B), while they believed that men, as well-formed shoots of noble genus, also possessed something divine, and as such could claim to approximate to divine stature — "the Godlike Agamemnon". In the nature of man himself, just as the deity wishes, lie possibilities, seemingly divine in origin, *diogenes*, and thus it is that every Indo-European people has readily tended to assume the incarnation of all aristocratic national values in human families, the *kalog'agathia*.[14]

Indo-European religiosity is not slavery, it contains none of the implorings of a downtrodden slave to his all-powerful lord, but comprises rather the confiding fulfilment of a community comprising Gods and men. Plato speaks in his *Banquet* (188 cc) of a "mutual community (*philia*) between Gods and men". The Teuton was certain of the friendship of his God, of the *astvin* or the *fulltrui* whom he fully trusted, and with the Hellenes in the Odyssey (XXIV, 514) the same certainty is found expressed in the words "friends of the Gods" (*theoi philoi*). In the *Bhagavad Gita* of the Indians (IV, 3) the God Krishna calls the man Arjuna his friend. The highest deity such as Zeus is honoured as "Father of the Gods and of men" — as a family father, as Zeus Herkeios, not as a despot. This idea is also expressed in the names of the Gods: Djaus pitar with the Indians, and Jupiter with the Romans. The name of the Indian God Mitra, which correspoirded to Mithra in Iran, means "friend". Mazdaism, founded by Zoroaster, called the morally acting man a friend of

Ahura Mazda, the One Universal God, who in the era of Achaemenides became the God of the Persian empire. According to Plato
(*Laws*, IV, 716) the man of moderation and self-control is above all
"a friend of God".

To the belief in the Gods as friends there thus corresponds the
Indo-European idea of kinship between the highminded and morally acting man and the Gods, which is already found in the 9th
Nemeian Ode of the Theban, Pindar. This kinship rests above all
on the view that Gods and men are bound through the same values,
through truth and virtue (Plato: *Laws* X, 899). This is also proclaimed
in the aforementioned Hymn to Zeus of Kleanthes of Assos, in
which Zeus is called the God "of many names", the God of *Logos*
(Reason), *Physis* (Nature), *Heimarmene* (Destiny), and the source of
all Becoming (Growth). Marcus Tullius Cicero, a pupil of Hellenic
wisdom (*de legibus* I, 25), also took over these ideas. From the same
ideas Plato deduced (Letter VII, 344A) that: "Whoever does not
feel inwardly bound to the just and morally beautiful ... will never
fully understand the true nature of virtue and vice".

In the Indo-European realm God is again and again regarded
as Reason ruling through world phenomena. Thus before Kleanthos
of Assos, Euripides (*Troades*, 884) in Hecabe's prayer equated Zeus
to the natural law and reason. The Stoics were convinced that the
same law of destiny bound both Gods and men, that therefore freedom for man was only possible as the moral freedom of the wise
man who had overcome his desires through rational insight. Here
Stoics have again expressed, what Buddha had already taught in
India centuries before, although both Stoics and Buddhists fell short
of pure Indo-European religiosity by rejecting and condemning
the world. Such reason (*Sapientia*) was also regarded by Cicero (*de
legibus* 1, 58) as the connecting link between Gods and men; to him
it was the "Mother of all Good", the priceless gift of the immortals
to mortals. An equation of God with reason was expressed by
Goethe towards the end of his life in a conversation with Eckermann
On 23rd February 1831, in which he described "the highest Being"
as "reason itself".

Paul distinguishes the religiosity of the Indo-Europeans from that of the Semites, when he asserts (I Cor. i. 22-23) that while the Hellenes strove for knowledge (*sophia*), the Jews desired revelations (*semaia*), and Aurelius Angustinus, the Bishop of Hippo (*Patrologiae cursus completes*, Vol. XXXVII, edited by J P Migne, 1845, SP. 1586; *ibid.*, Vol. XXVIII, 1845, SP. 1132) attempts by citing Bible passages, to disparage the wisdom (*sapientia*) of the Hellenes, alien to him as a Christian, as a folly before God and to find the highest wisdom only in the obedient humility (*humilitas obedentiae*) of the faithful.

The Indo-European belief in a coming together, almost a union, of God and man in reason which is common to both, can be called, in a derogatory manner, rationalism; but the Indo-Europeans have always tended to *logos* and *ratio* — to a *logos* and *ratio* which through fullness of knowledge is elevated far above the realm of arid good sense or dull hair-splitting. Indo-European thought has recognised and acknowledged a primacy of practical reason (Kant) which Marcus Tullius Cicero (*de legibus* I, 45) introduced by Posidonius to Hellenic philosophy — signified with the words: "The natural law undoubtedly states that the perfection of reason is virtue" (*est enim virtus perfecta ratio, quod certe in natura est*). Since Plato, Indo-European thinkers have taught that man could share or participate in the Good, the True and the Beautiful as partners of the divine. Indo-European thinkers (Duns Scotus, Schelling, Schopenhauer) are, each in his own way, driven through a voluntarianism beyond every rationalism.

But human intelligence and comprehension has its limits, while that of the deity is boundless, hence the Indo-Europeans, and particularly the Hellenes, have felt deeply their dependency on the Gods. The admonition "Know thyself!" which was inscribed in the vestibule of the temple of Apollo, reminded men of their limitations when faced with the deity. In his 5th Isthmian Ode (16) Pindar warned: "Do not strive to become Zeus!" The same experience of life and religion is found again with Goethe:

> *Denn mit Göttern*
> *soll sich nicht messen*
> *irgendein Mensch.*

For with the Gods
Shall no man measure himself

> (*Grenzen der Menschheit*)

The enticement to and danger of human self presumption was apparently familiar to the Indo-Europeans, perhaps for the very reason that they felt close to their Gods, and that when facing men of other races, they were conscious of their own superiority, and of their hereditary aristocratic qualities acquired by strict selection in the post ice-age millenia in central Europe. The fear of human hybris, of self overreaching, comes from the depths of the Hellenic soul, and in the face of all Hybris the limited man is admonished to keep to his ordained position in the timeless ordering of the world, into which the Gods also had to fit themselves. It is the Indo-European's destiny to stand proudly, and with an aristocratic confidence and resolution, but always aware of his own limitations, face to face with the boundlessness of the Gods — and no human species has felt this sense of destiny more deeply than the Indo-Europeans: the great element of tragedy in the poetry of the Indo-European peoples stems from the tension resulting from this sense of destiny.

Nevertheless it is completely impossible to conclude as W Baetke has done, that tragic destiny signified for the Indo-Europeans a ban or spell and brought about an anxiety of destiny, which made them ripe for a redemption. Not the God of Destiny, he claims, but the redeemer God brought the Teutons to the fulfilment of their religious longings.[15] Thus one can pass judgment concerning the Teutonic and Indo-European only externally, never from within outwards. The conversion of the Teutons to Christianity can only be explained by assuming that amongst them many men of softer heart could not withstand the gaze from the eyes of a merciless destiny and — against all reality — took their refuge in the dream image of a merciful God. Indo-European men of stronger heart have always been, like Frederick the Great, born Stoics, who standing upright like the devout Vergil, have recognised a merciless fate (*inexorabile fatum*).

H. R. Ellis Davidson (*Gods and Myths of Northern Europe*, 1964, p 218) has strikingly described the religiosity of the Scandinavians, whose Gods like men were subject to destiny: "Men knew that the gods whom they served could not give them freedom from danger and calamity, and they did not demand that they should. We find in the myths no sense of bitterness at the harshness and unfairness of life, but rather a spirit of heroic resignation: humanity is born to trouble, but courage, adventure, and the wonders of life are matters for thankfulness, to be enjoyed while life is still granted to us. The great gifts of the gods were readiness to face the world as it was, the luck that sustains men in tight places, and the opportunity to win that glory which alone can survive death."

CHAPTER THREE

IT is the spiritual strength of the Indo-Europeans — and this is witnessed by the great poetry of these peoples, and above all by their tragedies — to feel a deep joy in destiny — in the tension between the limitation of man and the boundlessness of the Gods. Nietzsche once called this joy *amor fati*. Particularly the men rich in soul amongst the Indo-European peoples feel — in the very midst of the blows of destiny — that the deity has allotted them a great destiny in which they must prove themselves. Goethe, in a letter to Countess Auguste zu Stolberg of the 17th July 1777 expresses a truly Indo-European thought, when he writes:

Alles geben die Götter, die unendlichen,
ihren Lieblingen ganz:
alle Freuden, die unendlichen,
alle Schmerzen, die unendlichen, ganz.

The eternal Gods give everything
utterly to their favourites,
all joys, and
all sorrows for all eternity — utterly and completely.

Never is this Indo-European joy in destiny turned into an acceptance of fate, into fatalism. When faced with the certainty of death the Indo-European remains conscious that his inherited nature is that of the warrior. This is expressed in the Indian *Bhagavad Gita* (XI, 38) by the God Krishna, when he says to Arjuna: "Joy and pain, gain and loss, victory and defeat, think on these things and array thyself for the battle, thus shalt thou bring no blame upon

29

thyself". And later the God characterises Indo-European nature still more dearly, when he (XVIII, 59) says: "When thou ... thinkest: 'I will not fight,' then this thy resolution is vain, thy aristocratic nature will drive thee to it".

This is the Indo-European view of destiny, the Indo-European joy in destiny, and for the Indo-Europeans life and belief would be feebly relaxed, if this spectacle were withdrawn in favour of a redeeming God.

Ideas of a redemption and of redeemers have, with the peoples of Indo-European tongue, only been able to spread in the late periods and then usually only amongst Indo-Europeanised substrates. When one wishes to apply a concept like redemption to the original nature of the Indo-European, one can speak at most of a self-redemption, but never of a redemption through a God-man, a demi-God or God. But Indo-European self-redemption should be described more correctly as self-liberation, as the liberation of the morally self-purifying soul, sinking through itself into its own ground of being, a liberation into the timeless and spaceless and a liberation from the necessity of existence and the necessity of being. Such a self-liberation, attained by overcoming the desires of the self (Pali: *kilesa=nibbana* or *tanhakkhaya*, the *apatheia* of the Stoics) was taught by the Indian prince's son, Siddhartha, the Wiseman with "eyes the colour of blossoming flax",[16] who later was called Buddha, the Illuminated.

Such a liberation from time and space is experienced in the Indo-European realm by the mystic as the Nirvana during lifetime, (Pali: *samditthika nibbana*), as the apartness or solitude of the individual soul sinking into itself, which experiences itself on its deepest ground as the universal soul or part of it. Hence the mysticism of the West may not be confused with a redemption.

The Indo-Europeans have always tended to raise the power of destiny above that of the Gods (cf. *Iliad*, 15, 117; 17, 198 ff. 22, 213; *Odyssey* III, 236 ff.; Hesiod, *Theogonia* 220; Aeschylus, *Prometheus* 515 ff.; Herodotus I, 91) especially, undoubtedly, the Indians, the Hellenes and the Teutons. The *Moira* or *aisa* of the Hellenes who already appeared in Homer and Heraclitus, corresponded to the

Norns of the Teutons, to the *wurd* (Weird, Wyrd; Scandinavian: Urd). In Shakespeare's *Macbeth* destiny (old English Wyrd) is represented by the Three Weird Sisters, who correspond to the *Parcae* with the Romans and as goddesses of destiny also appear with the Slavs in similar shapes,[17] while there was a goddess of destiny among the Letts (Latvians, an Indo-European Baltic people), who was called Leima. Even Plato (Laws V, 1741A) in the late period of his people, stressed that the deity was subject to destiny, and an Anglo-Saxon proverb, composed by a Christian poet, holds firm to the pre-Christian outlook: "Christ is powerful, but more powerful is destiny." Ahura Mazda, the god of heavens of the Iranians, distributes destiny as does Zeus, the heavenly God of the Hellenes (C. Widengren: *Hochgottglaube im alten Iran*, Uppsala Universitets Arsskrift, 1938, VI, p253 ff.); both, however, can do nothing against destiny. But I repeat, this Indo-European view of destiny has nothing to do with fatalism referring merely to that ultimate and hard reality, from an awareness of which Indo-European religiosity originates to rise Godwards. According to his whole nature the IndoEuropean cannot even wish to be redeemed from the tension of his destiny-bound life. The loosening of this tension would have signified for him a weakening of his religiosity.

The very fact of being bound to destiny has from the beginning proved to be the source of his spiritual existence. "The heart's wave would not have foamed upwards so beautifully and become spirit, if the old silent rock, destiny, had not faced it." This certainty, expressed by Hölderlin in his *Hyperion*, was presaged by the tragedies of Sophocles and of every great poet of Indo-European nature. It is the same certainty, which Schopenhauer has expressed in a hard remark: "A happy life is impossible, the highest to which man can attain is a heroic course of life" (*Parerga and Paralipomena*, Volume XI. Chapter 34)-

It is clear that a religiosity arising from such an attitude towards life can never become universal. Indo-European religions can never be transferred to other human breeds at choice. To them belongs *mahatma* (India), *megalethor* (*Iliad* XVI, 257; *Odyssey* XI, 85) *megalophron* or *megalopsychos* (Hellenic) (cf. Aristotle: *Nicomachian*

Ethics 7, 7, IV, 3, 1-34), *magnitude animi* (Ulrich Knoche: *Magnitudo animi*, *Philologus*, Supplementband XXVII, 3, 1935), *magnanimus* (Roman), the *mikilman* and the *storrada* (North German), of the ancient Nordic *mikilmenska* or *stormenska*, of the men of *hochgemüte* (lofty heart), as it was called in the German Middle Ages— all descriptions which could each be a translation of the other. Religiosity is here the maturing of the hero in the face of destiny, which he confronts alongside his Gods. This is also the meaning of Shakespeare's "Readiness is all" (*Hamlet* V, 2, 233) and "ripeness is all" (*King Lear* V, 2, 33).

It has been said that the Teutonic conception of life was a Pan-tragedy, an attitude which conceives all existence and events of the world as borne along by an ultimately tragic primal ground.[18] But this Pan-tragedy, which appears almost super-consciously with the true Teuton, Hebbel, is not solely Teutonic, and is found amongst all Indo-Europeans,[19] permeating all Indo-European religiosity. The Indo-European becomes a mature man only through his life of tension before destiny. The Teutonic hero, superbly characterised by the Icelandic Sagas, loftily understands the fate meeting him as his destiny, remains upright in the midst of it, and is thus true to himself. Aeschylus (*Prometheus Bound*, 936) commented similarly, when he said: "Wise men are they who honour Adrasteia", Adrasteia being a Hellenic goddess of destiny.

Because destiny signified so much to the religious Indo-Europeans, we find many names for it in their languages: the *Moira* of the Hellenes correspondes to the *fatum* of the Romans, the *ananke* and *heimarmene* of the Hellenes to the *necessitas* and *fatalitas* of the Romans. The Teutons named destiny according to the aspect from which they viewed it, as *orlog*, *metod*, *wurd*, *shuld* and *giskapu* (cf. also Eduard Neumann, *Das Schicksal in der Edda*, Beiträge zur deutschen Philologie, Vol. III, 1955). With the Indians the idea of destiny had become the idea of Karma, (cf. Julius von Negelein, in *Die Weltanschauungen des indogermanischen Asiens*, p 116, pp 165 *et seq.* Vol. I, 1924, pp 116 *et seq.* Veröffentlichungen des Indogermanischen Seminars der Universitit Erlangen) the idea of a soul migration which according to one's moral behaviour during lifetime invariably led to a better or worse life af ter reincarnation— a concept which was, however, peculiar to the Indians. The idea of a cycle of births, according to the description by the Hellenes of a *kyklos tes geneseoos*, was originally probably peculiar to all Indo-Europeans, and is also proved to have existed among the Celts and Teutons. (cf. also Erik Therman, in *Eddan och dess Odestragik* 1938, pp 133-134, 172). Perhaps it is also to be explained from the attentive observation of inherited bodily and spiritual features in the clans amongst the Indians as well as the Iranians, the Hellenes as well as the Romans and Teutons— for heredity, or having to be as one is, is destiny.

Erik Therman (in *Eddan och dess Odestragik* 1938, p 90) has found a "mocking defiance in the face of destiny, a struggle against this destiny despite recognition of its supreme power" to be characteristic of the *Edda* and many of the Icelandic tales. Such a defiance also still speaks from the Mediaeval *Nibelungenlied*, which astonished Goethe by its non-Christian character, which characterised Teutonic imperturbability in the face of merciless destiny. It was this same Indo-European imperturbability, which Vergil and even the mild Horace praised:

> *Felix qui potuit rerum cognoscere causas*
> *atque metus omnis et inexorabile fatum*
> *subiecit pedibus strepitumque Acherontis avari*
>
> (Georgica II, 490-492)

> *Si fractus illabatur orbis,*
> *impavidum ferient ruinae*
>
> (Carmina III, 3, 7-8).

Geibel also expressed the same idea in his *Brünhilde* (II, 2):

> *If there's anything more powerful than fate,*
> *then it's courage, which bears fate unshaken.*

I have mentioned above that the idea of destiny had already been reflected in Hellenic philosophy by Heraclitus, Plato and others. The Stoics, in particular, Posidonius, conveyed the Hellenic concept of a law of destiny (*heimarmene*) to the Romans, which was most dearly understood by Epicurus and his disciples Titus Lucretius Carus, Vergilius, Horatius.

The church has attempted to displace the Indo-European idea of destiny by the idea of providence (*providentia*). With thinking men the attempt failed, for thinking Indo-Europeans would not accept a providence, which blindly distributes an excess of grim blows of fortune, at the same time regarding this as love and benevolence. In Kant's *Opus Postumum* is found the remark— "If we wished to form a concept of God from experience, then all morality would fall away and only despotism be left." Therefore, concluded Kant, one would have to assume that such a creator of the world had no regard for the happiness of his creatures.

Whoever is of the same opinion as Baetke (a.a.0., p 33) or H. Rückert, that such views signify "no satisfactory solution to the question of destiny", or shares the allusion that these men were "never ready religiously to face the question of destiny",[20] — understands here as an outside observer, by the question of destiny something completely different from that resolute acceptance of destiny in which the Indo-European saw himself living. It is not by dissolving the question of destiny in the idea of redemption that the Indo-European can perfect his nature— for such redemption would probably appear to him as evasion; his nature is perfected solely through proving himself in the face of destiny. "This above all: to thine own self be true! " (*Hamlet* I, 3, 78). From the moral command to remain true to oneself, however, it again follows that Indo-European religiosity is of an aristocratic character: one does not advise the degenerate to remain true to himself.

Here I have not tried to provide any solution to the philosophic or religious question of destiny, but merely to explain how the Indo-European has lived in his destiny and how it has contributed to the maturity of his character.

The certainty of a destiny has not made the true Indo-European seek redemption, and even when his destiny caused him to tremble, he never turned to contrition or fearful awareness of "sin". Aeschylus, who was completely permeated by Hellenic religiosity and by the power of the divine, stands upright, like every Indo-European, before the immortal Gods, and despite every shattering experience has no feeling of sin.

Thus Indo-European religiosity is not concerned with anxiety, or self-damnation, or contrition, but with the man who would honour the divinity by standing up squarely amid the turmoil of destiny to pay him homage.

The German word *fromm*, meaning religious or devout, is derived from the stem meaning capable or fit, and is related to the Gothic *fruma*, meaning first, and to the Greek, *promos*, meaning furthermost. For the IndoEuropeans, religiosity showed itself as the will which revealed in the midst of destiny, before the friendly Gods, the fitness of the true-natured man who thus became all the more upright and god-filled the more shattering were the blows of destiny. In particular the best men and the truest matured are expected by the Gods to prove themselves on the anvil of destiny.

The defiant religiosity of Indo-European youth, which challenges destiny to test the strength of the young soul, has been stressed by Goethe in his poem *Promethcus*. Hebbel has also strikingly portrayed youthful Nordic Indo-European religiosity in the poem *To the Young Men*. Indo-European nature extends from such youthful religiosity outwards to the quieter, more devoted and fulfilled religiosity of the poem by Goethe, *Grenzen der Menschheit*.

CHAPTER FOUR

NEVER have Indo-Europeans imagined to become more religious when a "beyond" claimed to release them from "this world", which was devalued to a place of sorrow, persecution and salvation — to "a beyond" to which was attributed the fullness of joys, so that a soul fleeing "this world", must long for it all his earthly life.

The American religious scientist, William James, has contrasted the religion of healthy mindedness and the religion of the sick soul,[21] and Western examples of the religiosity of a sick soul may be found in Blaise Pascal and Sören Kierkegaard. Indo-European religiosity is healthy both in body and soul, and the God-filled soul after elevation to the divine achieves equilibrium in all the bodily and spiritual powers of man.

While non-Indo-European or non-Nordic religiosity, often breaks out all the more excitedly the more a religious man loses his equilibrium, the more he is in *ekstasis* or outside himself, the more the Nordic Indo-European strives for equilibrium and composure.

The Indo-European has confidence only in those spiritual powers which are to be experienced when the soul is in equilibrium, that is to say, in proportion and prudence.

He also mistrusts, all insight and knowledge and experience, which the believer acquires only in some state of excitement. It is extraordinarily characteristic of Indo-European nature, that with the Hellenes *eusebeia* (religosity) and *sophrosyne* (prudence) are often used in the same sense. In this the Nordic nature of true Hellenic religiosity is clearly seen, and results always in *aidoos*, that is to say, the shyness, or reserve of the worshippers. Religiosity expresses itself with these powerful resolute men in prudent conduct and noble reserve, which qualities alone become part of the fullness of the divine. Here the root of Indo-European religiosity is revealed to ethnological gaze: the religiosity of a farming aristocracy of Nordic race,[22] and of honest generations, possessed of a secure self-consciousness and an equally secure reserve, who dispassionately contemplated all phenomena, and who preserved balance and dignity even when facing the divine. In the form and character of Indo-European religion speaks the nobility of the Nordic farming aristocratic nature — all those *fides, virtus, pietas,* and *gravitas,* which, summarised as *religio,* corresponding to the Hellenic *aidoos* (reserve), also formed the essence of the true Roman, originating from Indo-European ancestors. To this, however, there is a limit, which has been repeatedly alluded to above: Indo-European religiosity owing to its origin and its nature, can never become common to everyone.

What Nietzsche, the sick man, called Great Health and what appeared to him as of such high value, namely nobility, both permeate the religious life of the Indo-Europeans. Whoever wishes to measure religiosity by the visible excitement of the religious man must find the Indo-Europeans irreligious. The highest attainments of Indo-European religions are only accessible to him when he has learned to master his spiritual powers in due proportion, and when he has achieved a proper sense of balance. Therefore Horace (*Carmina* II, 3, 1-2), in accordance with the wisdom of Hellenic teaching admonishes

> *Aequam memento rebus in arduis*
> *servare menteml*

As has been mentioned above (p 24), Plato described the man of moderation as a friend of the deity.

The Indo-European wishes to stand before the deity as a complete man who has achieved the balanced equilibrium of his powers which the deity demands from him.

A noble balance, the *constantia* and *gravitas,* which the Romans expected in particular from their senators and high officials, has also been found preserved, by one of the most eminent scholars of the pre-Christian Teutonic spirit, the Swiss, Andreas Heusler,[23] in the spiritual expression of the numerous Roman sculptures ' (Kurt Schumacher: *Germanendarstellungen*, edited by Hans Klumbach, 1935) of Teutonic men and women: "What strikes one most about these great, nobly formed features, is their mastered calm, their integral nobility, indeed their reflective mildness." But such spiritual features can also be recognised in the evidence of the ancient Teutonic moral teachings and wisdom of life which Andreas Hensler cites in the same connection. This evidence contradicts the slanders still sometimes repeated today that the Teutons were crude barbarians, to whom only the mediaeval church succeeded in inculcating moral standards.

The mastered calm and integral nobility mentioned by Heusler are, however, characteristics of the Indo-European in general, expressions of hereditary dispositions, which point back in time beyond the Teutonic into the Indo-European primal period, and thus into the early Stone Age of central Europe. This noble balance is the basis of Nordic religiosity: when facing the divine will the religious man preserves the equilibrium of his soul, the *acquanimitas* of the Romans, the *metriotes* and *sophrosyne* of the Hellenes, the *upeksha* of the Indians.

Hermann Oldenberg (*Buddha*, edited by Helmuth von Glasenapp, 1959, p 185) has described the peculiarity of Buddhistic religiosity as: "The equilibrium of forces, inner proportion — these are what Buddha recommends us to strive for". Buddha himself once compared the spiritual impulses of a religious man with a lute whose strings sound most beautifully of all when they are stretched neither too loosely nor too tightly (*Mahavagga* V, 1, 15-16). This and not perhaps a flaccid mediocrity is also the meaning of the *aurea mediocritas* of Horatius, which can be explained from the *Nichomachean Ethics* of Aristotle.

This ideal of integral nobility, common to all the Indo-Europeans, the sense of a noble balance has also expressed itself in works of the plastic arts and poetry. I have (p 15) cited the festival of the

Panathenaea, the *ara pacis* and the carmen *saeculare* of Horace as examples. In Athens every four years in celebration of the city goddess Athena, the all-Athenian (Pan-athenian) festival procession made its way to the Acropolis, as portrayed in the sculpture of the Parthenon frieze, one of the most beautiful creations of the noble balance of Hellenic and Indo-European religiosity. Ernst Langlotz, who wrote about this frieze in his book *Schönheit und Hoheit*, (p 14, 1948), describes the long series of these sculptures in such a way that through their noble self-control the tragic Indo-European destiny of the Hellenic is also recognised: these figures are "filled by the dangerous spiritual tensions of power in their life, which, akin to tragedy, elevates men, while it crushes them". Nobility of soul and calm, a calm which is above all expressed in the Parthenon, has also been described by Josef Strzygowski (*Spuren indogermanischen Glaubens in der Bildenden Kunst*, 1936, pp 279 *et seq*) as characteristic of Hellenic as well as of Indo-European nature in general.

The *ara pacis*, an altar dedicated in Rome in the year 9 BC probably based on Hellenic models and the Parthenon frieze, represents a sacrifice by noble Romans, in which Augustus himself and his family participates, accompanied by high officials and lictors. The architecture and its sculptures express the Hellenic-Roman religiosity of religion of *Aidoos* (reserve), even in this late period, in pure and mature shape.

The Roman poet Quintus Horatius Flaccus has also expressed pure and mature religiosity of an Indo-European type in the midst of a spiritually confused and morally desolate late period, in a festive religious poem, the *carmen saeculare* (*Carmina* III, 25). The Indo-European idea of world order, in which the man of belief strives to adapt himself, is here expressed again; Honour, manliness, loyalty, modesty and peace (Verse 57-58). The furtherance of all growth is implored from the Gods, the prospering of cattle and of the fruits of the fields; the Gods should present the Roman people "with success and children and everything beautiful" (Verse 45). The same attitude is evident in the greeting of the Scandinavian Teutons, who wished each other a fruitful year and peace (*ar ok fridr*) or also a fruitful year and prosperous herds of cattle (*ar ok fesaela*).

The upright man regards nothing in his nature as lower in value than deity; therefore for the Indo-Europeans there is no conflict between body and soul. This absence of conflict indeed already emanates from the will to preserve the equilibrium of the human powers, even when he conceives of the body and soul as different in essence. Yet on the whole the Indo-European has lived more in harmony of body and soul; the Teutons, for example, have always tended to regard the body as an expression of the soul.[24] A perceptive form of theoretical dualism, in which the subject faces the object — in which the perceiver faces an "object of perception" (H Rückert) — will be no more to the true Indo-European spirit, than a method, a convenient thought process for knowledge, and he will neither emphasise the concept of contrast between body and soul nor will he misjudge (as did Ludwig Klages) the spirit aroused in the tension between the subject and object as an adversary of the soul. To the Indo-European, the distinction between body and soul is not stimulating, not even to religiosity.

Thus this question has never vexed the Indo-Europeans, and they have never de-valued the body so as to value the soul more highly. Quite remote from them lies the idea that the body, addicted to this world, is a dirty prison for a soul striving out of it towards another world. Whenever the outer and inner in men are observed separately, then they are joined in the religious man in an effect of mutual equilibrium. The ideal of a healthy mind in a healthy body has become an English proverb in recent years, and in this we see the reassertion of Nordic religiosity in modern times. It is, after all, a reflection of the prayer which Plato, at the end of his *Phaedrus* causes Socrates to utter to the Gods:

"Grant that I may become beautiful within, and that my outward possessions do not conflict with the inner."

The honouring of the body as a visible expression of membership of a selected genus or race is characteristic of the Indo-Europeans. For this reason, every idea of killing the senses, of asceticism, lies very remote from this race, and would appear to them as an attempt to paralyse rather than balance human nature. It is something especially peculiar to the Hither-Asiatic race,[25] but it is also found in another form in the East Baltic race.[26] Indo-European religiosity is that of the soul which finds health and goodness in the world and in the body. For the religious men of the Hither-Asiatic race and for the western Europeans governed by the Hither-Asiatic racial spirit the Indo-Europeans must appear as children of this world, because the non-Indo-European spirit can seldom understand even the essence of Indo-European religiosity and hence will assume that it lacks religiosity altogether.

Hermann Lommel (*Iranische Religion*, in Carl Clemen, *Die Religionen der Erde*, 1927, p 146) uses the term "religiosity of this world" to characterise the Iranian (Persian) religion: "Life in this world", he says, "offered the Iranians unbounded possibilities for the worship of God". Goethe also, in his poem *Vermächtnis altpersischen Glaubens* has strikingly described the religiosity of the Iranians:

> *Schwerer Dienste tägliche Bewahrung,*
> *Sonst bedarf es keiner Offenbarung.*
>
> Daily preservation of hard services,
> No other kind of revelation is needed.

The Indo-Europeans are truly children of this world in the sense that this world can allow the unfolding of the whole richness of their worshipping, confiding and entrusting dedication to the divine, a worshipful penetration of all aspects of this life and environment through an all embracing elevated disposition of the mind. The divine is found to be universally present, as Schiller (*The Gods of Greece*) has described it:

> *Alles wies den eingeweihten Blicken,*
> *alles eines Gottes Spur.*
>
> To the enlightened, the whole Universe
> breathes the spirit of God.

Thus the religious forms of the Indo-Europeans have unfolded with great facility into a multiplicity of Gods, always accompanied, however, by a premonition or clear recognition that ultimately the many Gods are only names for the different aspects of the divine. In the worship of mountain heights, rivers, and trees, in the worship of the sun, the beginning of spring, and the dawn, (Indian *Ushas*, Iranian *Usha*, Greek *Eos* from *Ausos*, Latin *Aurora* from *Ausosa*, Teutonic *Ostara*), in the worship of ploughed land, and the tribal memory of outstanding individual leaders of prehistory subsequently elevated to the status of demi-Gods . . . in all this the Indo-European religiosity of "this world" is revealed as an expression of the experience of being sheltered and secure in the world which these peoples felt. W. Hauer[27] has described the foundation of the Indo-European religiosity as "being sheltered by the world" (*Weltgeborgenheit*). One could also quote Eduard Spranger (cf. p 17) in support of this when he spoke of the religiosity of this world in which this feeling of being secure in the world has been expressed.

Since being secure in the world forms the basis of this religiosity, as soon as it is developed with philosophic reflection it easily assumes the concept of the universal deity and becomes pantheistic, but this tendency remains reflective, and Indo-European religiosity never becomes intoxicated by the more impulsive forms of mysticism.

The strictly theistic religions of the Semites proclaimed personal Gods. T. H. Robinson (*Old Testament in the Modern World*, in H. H. Rowley: *The Old Testament and Modern Study*, 1951, p348) states categorically that "in the Jewish or Old Testament belief, there is no room left open for any kind of Pantheism." Arthur Drews, in *Die Religion als Selbstbewusstsein Gottes* (1906, pp 114-115), called Theism the basic category of Semitic religiosity, and Pantheism the basic category of Indo-European. Hermann Güntert, in *Der arische Weltkönig und Heiland*, (1923, pp 413 *et seq*.) found that mysticism corresponds to the Indo-European kind of mind, and considers that the existence of such a common tendency depends on their original racial identity.

The original Indo-European characteristically did not conceive of temples as dwelling places for Gods, nor did the oldest Indians.

The early Romans and the Italici probably neither built temples nor carved images of the Gods. Tacitus (*Germania* IX) wrote that the Teutons' idea of the greatness of the deity did not permit them to enclose their Gods within walls. For the same reason the Persian King Khshayarsha (Xerxes) burnt the temples in Greece (Cicero, *de legibus* II, 26: *quod parietibus includerunt deos*) which the Hellenes, deviating from the original Indo-European outlook, had begun to construct in the seventh century BC — wooden buildings at first, unmistakeably derived from central European early Stone Age and Bronze Age rectangular houses. Similarly the fact that the Indo-Europeans originally possessed no images of their Gods may correspond to a religiosity originating in the feeling of being secure in the world, and of being men of broad vision, an attitude which from the beginning has tended towards the concept of universal divinity.

The broad vision of the Indo-Europeans — a vision of man summoned to spiritual freedom, to *theoria*, or beholding (gazing) as perfected by the classical art of the Hellenes — such a vision comprehends the whole world, and all divine government and all responsible human life in it, as part of a divine order. The Indians call it *rita*, over which Mitra and Varuna (Uranos in Greek mythology) stand guard — "the guardians of *rita*",[28] the Persians call it *ascha* or *urto* (salvation, right, order); the Hellenes, *kosmos*; the Italici, *ratio*; the Teutons, *örlog*, or *Midgard*. Hermann Lommel, in *Zarathustra und seine Lehre*, Universitas XII Year, 1957, speaks of a "lawful order of world events", which the Iranians are said to have represented. Such an idea, the idea of a world order in which both Gods and men are arranged, permeates the teaching of the Stoics, and when Cicero (*de legibus* I, 45; *de finibus* IV, 34) praises virtue (*virtus*) as the perfection of reason, which rules the entire world (*natura*), then he once more expressed the idea of universal ordered life. This idea was recognised and expounded by the Jena scholar of jurisprudence Wilhelm Leist (1819-1906) in his works *Ancient Aryan Jus gentium* (1889) and *Ancient Aryan Jus civile* (1892-1896). Julius von Negelein in *Die Weltanschauungen des Indogermanischen Asiens*, (Veröffentlichungen des Indogermanischen Seminars der

Universität Erlangen Vol. 1, 1924, pp 100 *et seq*, 104 *et seq*, 118 *et seq*) has studied the idea of order as expressed in the course of the year with Indians and Iranians, an idea which corresponded to the teachings of the duty of the man of insight and of elevated moral outlook to fit himself into the order of the world. Later Wolfgang Schultz (*Zeitrechnung und Weltordnung*, 1929) stressed that it is found solely of all the peoples on earth, amongst the Indo-Europeans. The fragment of a Hellenic prayer has been preserved which implores the Gods for order (*eunomia*) on behalf of mortals (*Anthologia Gracca*, Vol. II, edited by Diehl, p 159).

In India the caste order also corresponded to universal order of life (Gustav Mensching, *Kastenordnung und Führertum in Indien*, Kriegsvorträge der Universität Bonn am Rh., Heft 93, 1942, pp 8 *et seq*). By means of the caste order, the three highest castes, descendants of the tribes which immigrated from the south-eastern middle Europe in the second pre-Christian millenia (R von Heine-Geldern: *Die Wanderungen der Arier nach Indien in archaeologischer Betrachtung* — (Forschungen und Fortschritte, Year 13, No. 26-27, p308; Richard Hauschild: *Die Frühesten Arier im alten Orient*) who, like the Iranians, called themselves Aryans, attempted to keep their race pure. The caste law was regarded as corresponding to the law of world order (*dharma*), or the *ius divinum* as the Romans described it. Participation in the superior spiritual world of the Vedas, Brahmanas and Upanishads originally determined the degree of caste. The higher the caste, the stricter was the sense of duty to lead a life corresponding to the world order. Jawaharlal Nehru (1889-1964), who can be described as predominantly Nordic from the shape of his head and facial features, informs us in his autobiography, that he originated on both his father's and mother's side from the Brahman families of Kashmir — from the mountainous north-west of India, into which the Aryans had migrated in substantial numbers, where blond children are still sometimes found — and that one of his aunts had been taken for an English woman because of her fair skin, her light hair and her blue eyes. All the great ideas of Indian religion and philosophy were either brought into India with the Aryan immigrants or else have originated in the area of Aryan settlement, that is in the valley of the Indus, the land of the five streams (the Punjab) or the region of the upper Ganges.

If in Germany there were a university chair to study the spiritual life of the Indo-Europeans, in the same way as in France there is a chair to study "la civilisation Indo-Européenne", at present occupied by the outstanding, though almost unknown, George Dumézil, then the interrelationships of the Indo-European spirit and interpretation of the world (B W Leist bravely attempted this study towards the end of the nineteenth century) would have been investigated more zealously. The idea which took shape in the Christian Middle Ages, of co-ordinating everything in this world to another world, extending from the division of the classes of the state to include the segregation of all men into an *ordo salutis*, an order of salvation, is probably a blend of thought derived from the impact of the Indo-European concept of the meaningful world order upon the invocation of Pauline-Augustinian Christianity to retreat from "this world". It is also interesting to find that Ernst Theodor Sehrt (*Shakespeare und die Ordnung*, Veröffentlichungen der Schleswig-Holsteinischen Universitatsgesellschaft, N.F., No. 12, 1955, pp 7 *et seq*) has shown that the Indo-European idea of order, linked with the Pythagorian and Platonic ideas of the harmony of the spheres and with the Stoic praise of reason, which is understood as in accord with world order, is also found in Shakespeare.

"The Gods fixed the measure and end of everything on mother earth," says the *Odyssey*, (XVIII, 592-593) and Pherecydes who was probably taught by Anaximandros speaks in the sixth century BC of ordering Zeus and here the idea of the divine world order resounds, just as it resounds in the *Edda* in The Vision of the Seeress:

> Then go the Regi rulers all
> To their judgment stools,
> These great holy Goths
> And counselt together that
> To the Night and New Moon
> They'd give these names.

> Morning also they named
> And Mid-Day too
> Dinner and Afternoon
> The time for to tell.

(*The British Edda*; L. A. Waddell 1930, p 23).

Family, nation and state, worship and law, the seasons of the year and the festivals, (cf. also Johannes Hertl, *Die Awestischen Jahreszeitenfeste*, Berichte über die Verhandlungen der Sächsischen Akademie der Wissenschaften, phil. hist. Klasse, 85Bd., Heft 2, 1933; *ibid. Das indogermanische Neujahrsopfer*, gleiche Schriftenreihe, 90.Bd., Heft 1, 1938) the customs and spiritual life, farmland, house and farm; all were related in a world order, and in this order man lived as a member of his race, which was perpetuated permanently in ordered procreation. This appears with the Hellenes as the Hestia idea, and was symbolised with all Indo-Europeans in the worship of the fire of the hearth (in Indian, *Agni*; in Latin *ignis*; in Iranian *Atar*; in Celtic, *Brigit*). Thus within the all-embracing world order, disciplined and selective procreation plays a divine role for the preservation of racial inheritance, the God-given racial heritage. Thus care of race is both a consequence and a requirement of the world order — a direct assertion of the Indo-European religious heart.

In the Indian *Law Book of Manu* X, 61, may be found the idea of order in procreation: "The inhabitants of the kingdom, in which disorderly procreation occurs, rapidly deteriorate". Hence the Indo-European holds sexual life sacred, enshrining it in the family and the woman, honouring the mistress of the house (*despoina, matrona*) as the guardian of their racial Heritage. The worship of the *divi parentes* sprang naturally from the pride and reverence in which they held their ancestors. It follows that Indo-European religiosity calls for disciplined choice (*Zuchtwahl*), in selecting a husband or wife, (a *eugeneia*) and that Indo-European families strive to preserve good breeding.

In the recorded cosmic or Mitgard concepts of the Indo-Europeans, man has his proper place in the great scheme of ordered life, but he is not enchained to it as are the oriental religions, with their star worship and priestly prophesies of the future — the study of entrails and the flight of birds, practised by the Babylonians, Etruscans and others. He appears in a trusting relationship with his God, whose nature itself is connected with the world order, and he joins with this God on a national scale in the struggle against all powers hostile to man and God, against chaos, against Utgard. The Indo-European recognises Mitgard, the earth-space, as the field in which he may fulfil his destiny, cherishing life as a cultivator or farmer, where plants, animals and men are each called to grow and ripen into powerful forces asserting themselves within the timeless order. Guilt in man — not sin — arises wherever an individual defies or threatens this order and attempts through short-sighted obstinacy to oppose the divine universal order in life. For such a crime an individual incurs guilt. By such a crime, his people are threatened with the danger of decline and degeneration, and the world order with confusion and distortion.

> *Wenn des Leichtsinns Rotte*
> *die Natur entstellt,*
> *huldige du dem Götte*
> *durch die ganze Welt!*

> If the frivolous mob,
> distort nature,
> Honour thou the God
> Through all the world!

> (Von Platen, *Parsenlied*)

The Indo-Europeans, and particularly the Iranians, have to struggle continuously between on the one hand, the divine will, which strives to shape and introduce order into nations for the enhancement of every living thing, and between, on the other hand, a will hostile to God, which brings disintegration and distortion of form and the destruction of all seed on the other. The God Ahura Mazda (*Ormuzd*) perpetually struggles against the anti-God Angra Mainju (*Ahriman*). Mitgard, the universal order of life, preserves and renews itself only through the brave and the constant struggle of men and Gods against the powers bostje to the Divine order, against Utgard. (cf. also Julius von Negelein, note S. 116 *et seq*). Mitgard is the product of the harmonious ordering of human honour[29] and the divine laws.

The ideas of *rita* and *ascha*, the *kosmos* and *ratio*, and the Mitgard idea of the Indo-Europeans reveal particularly dearly that Indo-European religiosity was rooted in a will to enhance life. It was a religious outlook by virtue of which man, with his great soul, sought to stand proudly beside God as *megalopsychos*, inspired by the truly Indo-European *magnitudo animi*, the *stormenska*, the mental elevation and magnanimity of the Icelanders, the *hochgemüte* of the medieval German knights. "Rüm Hart, klar Kimming" as the Frisian proverb says, is characteristic of the religiosity of the Nordic Indo-European farming aristocracy.

CHAPTER FIVE

IF we survey the whole field of Indo-European religiosity it is clear that much of what has been held in the Christian West as characteristic of the especially religious mind, will be found lacking in the Indo-European — lacking for those who seek to measure the Indo-European in terms of their own different religious stamp. Death can never be regarded by the Indo-European as a gloomy admonition to belief and religiosity. The fear of death, the threatened end of the world and the judgment of the dead have often been described as reasons for adhering to the narrow path of faith and morality. This is not true of the Indo-Europeans, for whom religiosity is a means to a fuller and wider life. As the *Edda* says:

> Bright and cheerful
> should each man be
> until death strikes him
>
> (*Edda*, Vol. II, 1920, p144.)

Death is a significant phenomenon of human life, but the strength of Indo-European religiosity is not based upon the contemplation or fear of death. Death belongs to the universal order of life. The Indo-European faces it in the same way as the best in our people do today. Because for the honest man perfect human life is already possible on this earth, through balanced self-assertion; because, in the order of the world the death of the individual is a natural phenomenon in the life or progression of the race, and because the beyond has no essential meaning in the life of the Indo-European, death has no influence on the Indo-European's beliefs or moral concepts, except as a reminder that the time allowed to the individual to fulfil his purpose and duties as a member of the race is limited.

It is striking how pallid and how unstimulating are the original Indo-European ideas of life after death, such as the kingdom of death, of Hades, or Hel as seen by the Teutons.[30] The Teutonic concept of Valhalla is scarcely of value here, being a late and exceptional development, derived less from religious disposition than from the poetic descriptive gift, of the Norwegian and Icelandic poets of the Viking era. It is also striking to find that no memories of Valhalla have been preserved in German sagas and fairy tales. Fundamentally, death for the Indo-Europeans meant the passage to a life, which in its individual features resembled life in the world of the living, only it was quieter, more balanced. The dead person remained part of the clan soul, in which he had shared when alive. He was at no time an unbridled individual, but always part of the existence over generations of a clan, inhabiting hereditary farms in the national homeland. As part of the clan soul individual death had no meaning for him. What concerned him in the kingdom of death was the welfare and prosperity of his clan, with its horses and cattle, fields and meadows. Achilles, when dead, asks Odysseus, who had penetrated into the underworld: "Give me news of my splendid sons!" (*Odyssey* XL, 492) and goes away "with great strides, filled with joy" when he has learned of "his sons' virtue" (XI, 539-540). As Paul Thieme (*Studien zur indogermanischen, Wortkunde und Religionsgeschichte*, 1952 pp46 *et seq*), has shown, the Indo-European ideas of a kingdom of the dead were originally less gloomy than the later Hellenic ideas of Hades or the Teutonic concept of Hel. In the Rigveda of the Indians, as in the Avesta of the Iranians and as with Homer, memories are preserved of the kingdom of the dead as a pleasant meadow, a cattle meadow (Rigveda) or a foal's meadow (Homer) separated from the land of the living only by a river. On such green meadows the dead are reunited with their ancestors. According to Hans Hartmann (*Der Totenkult in Irland*, 1952, pp 207, 208) the honouring of dead ancestors as well as the worship of fire and the sun in Celtic Ireland corresponds to North-Germanic, Italic, Tocharic and Indo-Iranian customs, and seems therefore to form part of common Indo-European customs. Corresponding word equivalents between the Celtic and Italic on the one side and the Indo-Iranian on the other are also found (Paul Kretschmer, *Einleitung in die Geschichte der griechischen Sprache*, 1896, pp125 *et seq*; J. Vendryès, *Les Correspondances de vocabulaire entre l'Indo-Arien et l'Italo-Celtique, Memoires de la Societé de Linguistique*, Vol. XX, 1918, p268, ff. 285). Indo-European religiosity in fact has never emphasised the death of the individual, for the world order is regarded as timeless. Despite the decline of whole eras shaken through guilt, there is no actual world's end, nor any dawn of a "Kingdom of God" transforming all things, in preparation for which many "Westerners" today retreat from the world to reflect upon their "last hour".

As long as the order of life is preserved by the efforts of man and God against the powers hostile to the divine, the idea of redemption is incomprehensible to the Indo-Europeans. Redemption from what — and to what other existence? Mitgard was not evil, and if one strove by brave, noble or moral action to keep the forces of Utgard at bay, there was no better life than that of friendship with the Gods by participating through balanced self-assertion in the universal order of life.

The true and original Indo-Europeans lack the figures of redeemers, the "heralds of salvation" and "saviours", who are so characteristic of the history of Egypt, Palestine, Syria, and the entire region from Hither-Asia to India. The earliest stirring of the idea of redemption, and the earliest figure of a redeemer, the *saoschyant*, amongst the peoples of Indo-European tongue is found with the Persians undoubtedly due to an admixture of Hither-Asiatic race and culture whom L F Clauss has aptly described as "redemption men". Also, aspects of the Teutonic God Balder belong to the saviour figures of Hither-Asia, most of all in the circle of the Babylonian Astarte legends and the ideas widely spread in the Orient of the dying and ever rising God.[31] Balder has rightly often been compared with Christ. He is a saviour figure, given new meaning by the Teutonic spirit, and is no more an original Teutonic God, than are the Vanir, from south-east Europe whose Hither-Asiatic features were reinterpreted in Teutonic forms. For the unfolding of religious feelings heralds of salvation were not necessary to the Indo-Europeans.

The concept of a redeemer who serves as a mediator between the divinity and man must also be alien to Indo-European religiosity; according to his own nature, the Indo-European seeks the natural direct way to God. For this reason a priesthood as a more sacred class, elevated above the rest of the people, could not develop amongst the original Indo-Europeans.[32] The idea of priests as mediators between the deity and men would have been a contradiction of Indo-European religiosity and instead of a rulership of priests there developed amongst the original Indo-Europeans the far-sighted, resolute state organisations of the Nordic-Indo-European kind. Comprising a community of farmer warriors, the idea of the state proceeded from the freedom and equality of the land-owning family fathers, who owned their hereditary farm as freemen (Greek *klaroi* or *kleroi*, Latin *heredia*). It sprang therefore from a rural democracy, which in later times was usually succeeded by a city trading democracy. Democracy based on the rural spirit of yeomen has been celebrated by Gottfried Keller in *Fähnlein der sieben Aufrechten* (1861), while democracy based on the city-trader spirit was pilloried by him in *Martin Salander* (1896). The democracy of yeomen, by its very nature, did not permit the existence of a priestly hierarchy. Such other functions as a priestly hierarchy might desire to usurp were already fulfilled by the father of the family and the heads of the clans, tribes and nations in their natural and national function as a part of the world order.

It is true that the Indo-European might accept the priest as an interpreter and perfecter of the traditional folk spirit, as the unfolder and new creator of hereditary religiosity; that is in accordance with Indo-European nature. But the idea of the priest as a prophet, anxious to dominate and spiritually enchain the religious community, is something which Indo-European nature cannot tolerate, for Nordic-Indo-European religiosity is based on noble, measured conduct and the secure maintenance of a bodily and spiritual distance between men. Both heightening oneself, and emotional intoxication, *ekstasis,* or holy *orgia*, and standing outside oneself and the infiltration of self into the spiritual domains of other men, are distinctive features of the Hither-Asiatic race soul. Measure (balance), Yoga (Latin *iugum*, German *Joch*, English *Yoke*), *metron, temperantia*, are as above, distinctive features of the Nordic race soul and of the original Indo-European religiosity: *eusebeia* synonymous with *sophrosyne*; Sanscrit *upeksha*, Pali, *upekha*; likewise in the religiosity of the Stoics (*apatheia*) and of the Epicureans (*ataraxia*).

This is not to suggest that the Indo-Europeans were not aware that the condition of intoxication is indicative of superabundant spiritual activity — as distinct from alcoholic intoxication, which like the nectar of the Hellenes or the Met (Mead) of the Teutons they prepared from honey, and known by the Indo-Aryans as *Soma* and the Iranians as *Haoma*. From Herodotus (I, 33) and from Tacitus (*Germania* XXII) it can be seen that the Indo-Europeans demanded control of any state of intoxication. The sense of intoxication of the spiritual creator when finding and shaping new knowledge is admittedly to be traced amongst all peoples of Indo-European tongue, the *mania musoon*, the craze of the Muses without which, according to Plato, there is no spiritual creation. Without this "madness", the creations, re-creations and new creations of Indo-European religiosity would not have been possible. But when one seeks to ascertain to what extent the Indo-Europeans have expressed such spiritual intoxication in visible behaviour and in words, again and again one becomes aware of their self-control (*yoga, enkrateia, disciplina*, self-control.) Such intoxications allow the spirit to take flight, but the flight itself obeys the laws of race soul striving for balance. Hölderlin knew the "uncontrolled powers of Genius" but as a basic principle of creation he taught the Indo-European to seek the wisdom of a maturer age: "Hate intoxication like the frost!" he said, to which he added the admonition, "Be devout only as the Greeks were devout!" In this he echoed the words of Horace (*ars poetica* 268-269), expressing the awe aroused in men by the works of Hellenic poetry:

> *vos exemplaria Graeca*
> *nocturna versate manu, versate diurna!*

If we ask ourselves what the Hellenic spirit and what Hellenic art signified to Horace, to Winckelmann, Goethe, Wilhelm Von Humboldt, Hölderlin, and Shelley, then it must have been this: that among all Indo-European peoples, it was granted to the Hellenes to represent with the greatest clarity and beauty the balanced dignity of man in fearless freedom of the spirit. Walter F Otto (*Das Wort der Antike*, 1962, p 345) has described the impression — attractive to the Indo-European nature — which strikes visitors to a museum of ancient art when they pass from the Egyptian or Hindoo or east-Asiatic displays into the room of Hellenic art: "The first feeling one receives," he writes, "is that of a wonderful freedom." With such a feeling of freedom as this, the Hellenic man of balance and dignity confronted the deity.

What such Indo-European freedom signifies in the state will be studied later. Here we can only allude to what Cornelius Tacitus wrote: Freedom (*libertas*) in the Indo-European sense is only possible where a people strives to achieve the value of *virtus*, the dignity of the powerful, upright individual man. If in a people the freedom of the city masses, who desire welfare (Bread and Circuses) from the State, triumphs then in such a state the freedom of the individual man and that of the minority will be steadily suppressed by the majority, until finally only *dominatio* is still possible, that is to say, the equal subjection of all under one tyrant.

Confronted with the hereditary disposition of the Indo-Europeans, religions which have been described as revelations or stipendiary religions, ie religions with a "founder" were unable to develop among them. The sudden transformation of one's own nature into something completely different, the transformation which is regarded as a re-birth or inner experience belongs far more to the oriental race soul of the desert, and readily occurs in the Orient, where the predominant spirit is of the HitherAsiatic and Oriental races.[33]

Revelation — L F Clauss calls the Oriental race "revelation men" — the forming of religions through a prophet, the excitability and impulsiveness of the faithful for the revealed faith, are all phenomena which do not prosper in the realm of Indo-European religiosity. The elevation of faith in itself, and of credulity for the sake of credulity, the meritoriousness of faith as a particularly powerful magical means for justification before God — Luther's *sola fide* — religious manifestations such as these appear to the Nordic-Indo-Europeans as a distortion of human nature, of that human nature which is willed by the deity itself. Faith in itself cannot be an Indo-European value, but it is certainly a value for men of Oriental (desert land) races. Goethe in his introductory poem to the *Westöstlichen Divan* typified the overexcess and excitedness of Oriental faith and the lack of thought corresponding to such excess, being all "Broad belief and narrow thought". Excitedness for a belief, excitedness over an urge to convert, the mission to "unbelievers" the assertion that one's own belief alone could make one blessed, an excitedness, further, which expresses itself in hatred towards other Gods and persecution of their believers: such excited rage or fanaticism has repeatedly emanated from tribes of predominantly Oriental race and from the religious life of such tribes. Eduard Meyer, in his *Geschichte des Alterums* (1907, Part I, Book I, p 385), has even spoken of the brutal cruelty, which has distinguished the religious spirit of peoples of Semitic language.

All this is as remote and unnatural to the Indo-European as is the immersion of the self into alien domains of the soul, frequently evident in men of Hither-Asiatic race. The more convinced the Indo-European lived in his belief, all the more repellent to his nature must have been the idea of its being represented to a stranger as the only valid one before God. The Indo-European religiosity does not preach to non-believers, but is willing to explain to an enquirer the nature of his personal beliefs. Hence the patience of all Indo-Europeans in religious matters. In my book *Die Nordische Rasse bei den Indogermanen Asiens*, p 112, 1934), 1 have written: "Zeal to convert and intolerance have always remained alien to every aspect of Indo-European religiosity. In this is revealed the Nordic sense of distance between one man and another, modesty which proscribes intrusion upon the spiritual domains of other men. One cannot imagine a true Hellene preaching his religious ideas to a non-Hellene; no Teuton, Roman, Persian or Aryan Brahman Indian, who would have wished to "convert"other men to his belief. To the Nordic race soul, interfering in the spiritual life of other men is as ignoble as violating individual boundaries." Mutual tolerance of religious forms is a distinctive feature of the Indo-European. The memorial stones in the Roman-Teutonic frontier region reveal through their inscriptions that the Roman frontier troops and settlers not only honoured their own Gods, but also respected the local deity of the Teutons, the *genius huius loci.*

In the Persian kingdom of the Achaemenides, *Ahura Mazda* was worshipped as the Imperial God (G Widengren, in *Hochgottglaube im Alten Iran,* Uppsala Universitets Arsskrift 1938, pp 259 *et seq*) and from being an Iranian tribal God became God over all peoples of the earth.

Jahwe (Jehovah), who was originally a Hebrew tribal God, subsequently turned for many — not all — Jews into a God of all the peoples. But the Persians, as Indo-Europeans, never forced *Ahura Mazda* on the alien tribes and peoples of their kingdom. The kings Cyrus the Great and Darius passed commandments concerning the mutual tolerance of the religions of their Empire (G Widengren, *Iranische Geisteswelt,* Vienna 1961, pp 245 *et seq*). The Indian King Asoka, who was converted to Buddhism, the sole religion which spread peacefully and without bloodshed, ruled in approximately the middle of the third century BC in India over a great kingdom, and introduced laws prescribing mutual tolerance between the religions of his kingdoms. They were engraved on stone tablets, and many were rediscovered at the beginning of the nineteenth century. The historian can only cite such examples from the Indo-European realm. Vergil's law of sparing the vanquished (*parcere subjectis*) was practised by the Romans not only on subject peoples, but also on their Gods and religions although an *interpretatio Romana* once attempted to include alien Gods as being off-shoots of their own deities.

Ammianus Marcellinus, a troop leader in the army of the Emperor Julian, whom the Christians called the Apostate (*apostata*) wished to continue the histories of Tacitus in his own writings. In recording the events in his time, when Christianity had already become the state religion, Ammianus — a pagan — reported the intrigues of the Christians against Julian without abuse, since this would not have corresponded to his Hellenic-Roman attitude of tolerance. In the controversies of Pagan and Christian writers and poets, passionate worshippers of the old Roman belief such as Quintus Aurelius Symmachus, Ambrosius Theodosius Macrodius and Claudius Rutiliu Namantianus, have given their opinion of Christianity and Christians in dignified manner. Abuse and contempt for opponents is found in these times only amongst the Christian writers. Only after their conversion to Christianity, whose idea of God corresponded to the intolerant, religious war-waging Gods of the Semitic tribe, have Indo-European peoples forced their beliefs on alien tribes; the king of the Franks, Charlemagne forced Christianity upon the Saxons who were subjected after a bloody struggle. King Olav Tryggveson of Norway (995-1000), after being baptised in England, was persuaded to force conversion on his own people by cunning, treachery and cruel persecutions, as well as by bribing them to submit to baptism. Andreas Hensler (*Germanentum*, 1934, pp 47, 48, 119, 122) has asserted that among the Northern Teutons there was quite enough violence, but never cruelty; only after the introduction of Christianity did converted zealots behave cruelly towards their countrymen. With the conversion of the North, an alien wave of cruelty entered the land. Hensler has said that the methods of torture used by the converted King Olav against those who were reluctant to change their faith, could have been learned by the Northerners "only in the Orient".

Only in Iceland, whence many Pagan Norwegian yeomen fled from religious persecution to found a state of free and equal landowning family fathers, a characteristic Teutonic democracy, was the inherited tolerance restored and preserved. In this country alone was the Pagan faith permitted to survive without persecution after the triumph of Christianity — as recorded in the poems of the *Edda* and the long series of tales of the Icelanders, the Sögur (singular: Saga; cf Andreas Hensler: *Germanentum*, 1934, p94; Hans Kuhn: *Das Nordgermanische Heidentum in den ersten christlichen jahrhunderten*, Zeitschrift fur deutsches Altertm und deutsche

Literatur, Vol. LXXIX, 1942, p166). Even the heroic songs of Teutonic antiquity which had been collected and recorded by the Christian Charlemagne king of the Franks, were burned as being pagan by his son, Ludwig the pious. Indo-European belief without tolerance is inconceivable, and any Indo-European religious form, which demanded "true believers", is similarly inconceivable, just as much as an Indo-European form of belief in conflict with free research, and independent thought is inconceivable. Where excitedness of belief might damage the inborn love of truth and the inborn nobility of the freeman, rightness of belief cannot be considered as a value of religiosity. All Indo-European forms of belief, so long as they maintained the pure, traditional Nordic spirit, have remained free from any rigid doctrine of belief or dogma and from the worship of a revealed word. Hence it follows that under the original Indo-Europeans there arose no teachers to instruct the people in their beliefs, no theologians, and no priesthood holier and more elevated than the rest of the people. In this respect it is also a fact that Indo-European religious communities have never become churches. The churchifying of a belief is again an assertion of the spirit of the Oriental (desert lands) race or of the joint effect of Oriental and Hither-Asiatic race spirit.

There is yet another reason why no church could arise amongst the Indo-Europeans. A church as a sacred and sanctifying device for a community of men practising their special form of religiosity under priestly dominance, of men who desire to justify themselves before the deity — such a church can only take root, where "this" world is regarded as "unholy" and enticing to "sin". The result of the creation of such a church was to institute a separate holy region of the devout, a device to redeem hereditary sinful man (original sin) from the constriction of "this world" through its merciful means and to reveal a way of salvation to redemption.

But where the world consists of ordered life and the deity itself has joy in the justified man, the church as such has no meaning.

> Pay homage to the God
> through the whole world!

> (Von Platen).

Communion of belief will not therefore be shaped by the Indo-Europeans into a community with a special, rigid religious outlook. The formation of a community in this sense is opposed by the originality of the Nordic race soul of the individual Indo-European nations. "They live for themselves and apart" (*colunt discreti ac diversi*) said Tacitus (*Germania*, 16), describing the Teutonic manner of settlement. More than a habit, it is indeed an expression of the spiritual nature of the Teuton, of the Teutonic joy in the mutual retention of distance between men. In this frame of mind a taciturn, confiding community of belief is possible, but not the formation of a community upon which a spirit can descend, in whose tension all individual human nature consumes itself.

The Brahmanism of the Aryan Indians like the Druidism of the Celts, is an exception among the priesthoods of the Indo-European peoples, but it only developed as such over the course of the centuries, reflecting alien admixtures, customs and influences.

Indo-European religiosity will never be able to unfold in its purity in a church-community but certainly in a State whose structure is in accordance with the racial nature. In the "Gau" region of the Teutons, in the *civitas* of the Romans, in the *polis* of the Hellenes, ie in those folk orders in which Indo-European men organised their nation-states along lines peculiar to their own disposition, Indo-European religiosity has been able to develop in the purest of all forms. The individual Indo-European removed himself apart from men when he wished to pray (cf. *Odyssey* XII, 33), in contrast with the practice of the Semitic peoples, for whom prayer was a communal rite.

But in Xenophon's *Oikonomikos* (XI, 8), an official state prayer is mentioned, which implores of the Gods to send down on them "health, bodily strength, understanding between friends, salvation in war and well-being". Here the community of belief is a national not a religious community, and in such a kingdom Indo-European religiosity flowers to perfection.

Inborn Indo-European religiosity will unfold much more easily in a definite mystical form than in belief in redemption and revelation or in churchly forms. What causes the Indo-Europeans to show interest in mystical views, is the possibility of direct relationship with the deity, the deepening of an ever vital urge to "reciprocal friendship between Gods and men" (Plato) and the implicit tendency towards the ideas of the universal deity (Pantheism). The idea of miraculous creation is alien to the Indo-European, and particularly in mysticism the idea of creation falls away. Mystical outlooks have easily grown out of the Indo-European; with the Indians in the Vedas and Upanishads, in Brahmanism, in Buddhism, with Hellenes in the expositions of Platonic thought which incorporated Plato's *anamnesis* in the mystical sense though weakened and alienated by oriental spirit in the thinking of Plotinus and his neo-Platonic followers in the Middle Ages. Where Indo-Europeans accepted alien beliefs, mystical thought has later set in against these beliefs, as is already found with the Christian Boethius (480-525), who in his work, *Concerning consolation through philosophy*, advances viewpoints which he had taken over from Plato, the Stoics, the Neo-Pythagorians, and from Plotinus rather than from Christian services. The same mystic revolt, tending towards a return to Pantheism, is found in the Sufism which arose amongst the Aryan Persians after their forcible conversions to Islam. It also began to stir in Europe as soon as the Nordic-Teutonic spirit began to express itself against the Roman-Christian belief. Meister Eckhart, possibly represents most strongly the development of the mysticism as a result of the revolt of the Teutonic Indo-European spirit against Roman-Christianity.

CHAPTER SIX

BUT Indo-European religiosity is not able to unfold truly in conformity with its nature in every form of mysticism; not for instance, in the mysticism of supersensual and sexual moods and abandonments: not in the mysticism of intoxicated excitement, in that enthusiasmos, in which man wishes to torture himself out of the bounds of his body in order to reach down into the essence of the deity; nor also in the manner of being enraptured or carried away, as in Islamic mysticism by the feeling of being torn away, overpowered by a transcendent God, by the mysticism which involves a dissolution of all barriers, an immersion and swimming in formless unbecoming. All such trends are opposed to the Indo-European view of the ordered shaping of the world and the Indo-European feeling of duty to battle against destructive powers, against Utgard. Therefore the mysticism of self-seclusion (myein), of retreat from the world, of inaction and the extinction of the will or even of the senses, of excessive contemplation, the so-called quietistic mysticism — is not the mysticism of the Indo-Europeans. However much as calmness may be valued by the Indo-Europeans, deep as the insight he will acquire again and again in self-immersion or in the pure contemplation of things without activity of will, the Indo-European can never give himself up to them entirely, and self assertion, the confrontation of destiny, is essential to his nature. Indo-European mysticism is thus the inner contemplation of high-minded (*hochgemüter*) men: through sinking the morally purified individual soul (Indian *atman*) into itself, the soul experiences itself in its ground as the universal soul (Indian *brahman*).

For this reason Indo-European mysticism as inward contemplation will confine itself again and again to contemplation
which is unbounded in space — not secluded within itself, but
open, and far seeing, such as is represented most beautifully of all
through the far-aiming gaze of the Apollo of Belvedere, by whose
statue Winckelman was so moved and which he described so
stirringly! With such vision the Indo-European experiences the
divine:

> *Von Gebirg zum Gebirg*
> *schwebet der ewige Geist*
> *ewigen Lebens ahndevoll.*
>
> (Goethe, *An Schwager Kronos.*)

> From mountain to mountain,
> Hovers the eternal spirit
> of everlasting life ominously.

At great moments, Indo-European nature thus participates in a
vision, a *theoria*, a one and all (*hen kai pan*) in the All-one, which is
already taught by the older Upanishads in India[34] and then — each
in his own way — by the great early Hellenic thinkers, such as
Heraclitus, Xenophon and Parmenides.[35] A universal teaching of
Indo-European kind, the Vedanta philosophy,[36] was announced
in India at the beginning of the ninth century A.D. by the Brahman
thinker, Sankara. Since it came to be known in Europe and North
America it has influenced many thinking men. The same religiosity
breaks through Christian dogma in the Nordic-German mysticism
of reality, which H. Mandel has described.[37]

The wide vision of the Indo-European, which was represented
most beautifully of all through far-aiming Apollo, can develop into
a dedication to a universe without beginning and without end such
as Heraclitus announced, or it can emerge as that feeling of identity
with the universe which has been described as nature mysticism.
Joseph Strzygowski (in *Die Landschaft in der nordischen Kunst*, p 256)
has described the plastic art of the Indo-European as the "feeling"
of being one with the universe and its expanse. In such nature
mysticism the Indo-European width of vision and inner contem-

plation are combined. Western (ie European) landscape painting, above all that of the Teutonic peoples, and landscape lyricism,[38] above all in England and Germany, but also in Hölderlin's *Hyperion* display the same feeling of identity with Nature.

From the Indo-Iranian belief in the Gods of antiquity (polytheism), Spitama Zarathustra created in approximately the ninth century BC the first teaching of and belief in One God (Monotheism) in the history of religions. The Gods who had been common to the Indians and Iranians now passed into the background behind the one Ahura Mazda, after whom Mazdaism is named. These other Gods, preserved in India, in Iran became the sacred immortals (*amesha spenta's,*) the representatives of the moral virtues. They were later regarded as the messengers (Greek: *angeloi*) of Ahura Mazda, and the archangels created by Jewish and Christian legends were modelled on them. Spitama Zarathustra erected his monotheistic form of belief in a one-sided way, purely based upon morality, but in so doing be contradicted hereditary Indo-European religiosity. Hermann Lommel (*Von arischer Religion*, Geistige Arbeit, Year 1, No. 23, pp5-6) has proved, however, that, arising from Iranian popular belief, a natural religiosity again and again broke out in Mazdaism. A curious example of these outbreaks was the creation by the Persian kings, of landscape parks and gardens, whose fame spread far and wide. One of these gardens was called *pairidesa* and from it derived the Old Testament idea of Paradise and of the Garden of Eden (Josef Strzygowski: *Spuren Indogermanischen Glaubens in der Bildenden Kunst*, 1936, pp 279 *et seq*; Geo Widengren, *Hochgottglaube im Alten Iran*, Uppsala Universitets Arsskrift, 1938: 6. pp 151 *et seq* and 171 *et seq*, 372 *et seq*, 235, 240 *et seq*; A T Olmstead, *History of the Persian Empire*, 1952, pp 20, 62, 170, 315, 434; PAJ Arberry, *The Legacy of Persia*, 1953, pp 5, 35, 260-261, 271). According to Xenophon (*Oikonomikos*; IV, 20-22), the younger Kurash (Cyprus) who later fell in the battle of Kunaxa (401 BC), showed the Spartan Lysandros (Lysander) with pride his Paradise (paradeisos), a park laid out according to his plans with rows of beautiful trees, part of which he had planted himself.

Nature religiosity has also been expressed in Iranian poetry and plastic art in the descriptions of the "Landscape filled with the glory of the deity" (*khvarenah*), Josef Strzygowski: *Die Landschaft in der nordischen Kunst*, pp143, 261 *et seq*), akin to that of Indo-European aristocratic farmers, and the landscape parks of eighteenthcentury Europe.

It was Nature religiosity that filled the Persian king Khshayarsha (Greek: Xerxes), from the family of the Achaemenides, the king with the "flashing dark blue eyes" (Aeschylus: The Persians, 81) Herodotus (VII, 31) reports that, when on the march to Lydia and the Hellespont, the king caught sight of a beautiful plane tree, he had it hung with golden jewellery and guarded by a man from his bodyguard. This story called forth the famous Largo by Friedrich Handel, which was not, as generally assumed, a church composition, but a further example of Indo-European nature religiosity — the Persian king of Handel's opera *Serse* (Xerxes) praises the beautiful plane tree in song in the Largo *Ombra mai fu: o mio platano amato!*

Bismarck and Moltke were talking one day in Berlin after the war was ended in 1871 and Bismarck asked the field marshal what, after such events and successes, they could still enjoy in life together. After a pause, Moltke said simply, "to see a tree growing". The love and worship of trees as Erik Therman (*Eddan och dess Ödestragik*, 1938, pp124 *et seq*, cf also Giacomo Devoto, *Origini indoeuropee*, 1961, pp 251-52) has also shown was one of the characteristics of Teutonic religiosity.

Nature religiosity, the religiosity of aristocratic Indo-European farmers, also permeates the *Georgica* of Vergilius Maro (Vergil), the works of the painters Claude Lorrain and William Turner, Gottfried Keller's poetry and his novel *Der grüne Heinrich*, and the novel *Nachsommer* by Adalbert Stifter. Inborn nature mysticism has again and again removed far away from the teachings of the church many Christian theologians, as for example the Weimar court chaplain, Herder. The North American, Ralph Waldo Emerson (1803-82), resigned his office as pastor, when he could no longer reconcile the mystical concept of a world soul, which was revealed to him in the sublimity of landscape and in the demands of conscience, with the teachings of the church. His apologia, entitled *Nature*, appeared in the year 1836.

A surrender to the Cosmos, which on account of its being without beginning and end, cannot be called creation, a devotion to liberation from time and space, thus a Nirvana during lifetime, was experienced by Richard Jefferies (1848-1887), an English mystic, whose life and work, *The Story of my Heart*, has remained almost unknown in his own country.

Nature mysticism — contrary to the intention of the author, who thought in materialistic terms under the influence of Epicurus — can be seen, in the rich and grandiose poem of the Roman, Titus Lucretius Carus, *De rerum natura*. Even his introductory invocation to the Goddess Venus, in whom, however, Lucretius, as the heir to rational Hellenic thought, no longer believed, signifies more than mythological embellishment: it begets a spiritual fullness of poetry, a *hen kai pan*, a *unio mystica*, of the discerning poet and thinker with the universe as the object of his knowledge. The remoteness of a mystic also corresponds to the Roman poet's moral and religious goal: "to be able to view everything with a calm spirit" (V, 1203) — *pacata posse omnia mente tueri*.

Otto Regenbogen (*Lucretius: Seine Gestalt in seinem Gedicht, Neue Wege zur Antike*, Heft I, 1932, pp 47, 54, 61, 75 ff, 81 ff, 85 *et seq*) has shown that the Epicurian thinker Lucretius and the poet Lucretius were not one and the same person; but *De rerum natura* provides sufficient proof of the fact that Lucretius had departed from the materialist Epicurus and his teaching on the motions of atoms — apart from the fact that the Roman's poem was Stoic in spirit and more austere and manly, indeed more commanding, than the teaching of the Hellenic thinker. If Lucretius rejected all *religio* in general, then this is explained by the fact that the rural religiosity which originally formed the *religio* of the Latin-Sabine Romans, had already been penetrated, through the influence of the neighbouring Etruscans, with many gloomy superstitions and repellent customs. However, such a rejection of every religion speaks, as Regenbogen has said, more respect for the highest and ultimate things, than all the religious receptiveness of the philistine.

Was Lucretius a materialist as well as a nature mystic?

Goethe, the poet of nature religiosity (and as such not a materialist), was going to write a study of Lucretius in which he intended to portray him as a "natural philosopher and poet" (Goethe: *Von Knebels Translation of Lucretius*, Cotta's Jubilee edition, Vol. XXXVII, p 218), and he took an active interest in the translation by his friend Karl Ludwig von Knebel, who had made a masterly rendering of *De rerum natura* into German. Karl Büchner (*Römische Literaturgeschichte*, 1962, pp 236, 246, 249) has pointed out that Lucretius was the first Roman thinker to discover the spirit (*mens*), a spirit which liberates through knowledge: Lucretius discovered meaning "only in the superiority of the perceptive spirit", and that liberation could be achieved solely by belief in the "power of the spirit and of reason". Liberation to the timeless value of "a firm, lasting spirit" was the religious and moral goal of the poet. *Genus infelix humanus* (V, 1194) the unfortunate species of humanity, was looked on by the poet as men who were still bound by superstition, incapable of attaining the freedom of the spirit.

But if Lucretius the thinker thus portrayed for the Romans the capacity of perception, the spirit (*mens*), then Lucretius the poet, in contrast to Epicurus, who in his nature teachings had proceeded from Democritus, must have had a premonition or have understood that while feeling (sensitivity), consciousness and the perceptive activity of man were linked to the material activity of the brain and body and hence, in the last analysis, as Democritus and Epicurus had taught, to the movements of atoms, yet they were not in fact derived from such movements, and cannot be explained by them. Spirit becomes alive only in the tension between a discerning (perceptive) consciousness which faces, as Subject, an Object of perception. While Lucretius the Epicurean followed the materialistic atomic teaching of the Hellene, the poet Lucretius discovered a spirit which is free to experience natural religiosity. It is worth commenting here that Walter F Otto (*Das Wort der Antike*, 1962, pp 293 *et seq*) also regarded both Epicurus and Lucretius as poets of a religious mind.

In Faust's monologue in the scene "Wald und Höhle" (*Faust* I,

Verse 3217, *et seq*) Goethe has linked both with each other: the study of the Object Nature, in the sense of Lucretius the thinker is linked in antithesis with a sensitive and discerning consciousness as Subject namely — the "secret, deep miracles in one's own breast" (Verse 3232 *et seq*) — giving rise to a power of reflection without which a true understanding of magnificent Nature cannot be grasped. With Goethe, it is not possible, as with Lucretius, to separate the poet from the thinker. But Goethe, like his friend Knebel, was enthused by the latter's natural religiosity which he expressed in his Poetry and Truth (Second part, sixth book, *Goethe's Complete Works*, Cotta's Jubilee edition, Vol. XXIII, p 10): "God can be worshipped in no more beautiful way than by the spontaneous welling-up from one's breast of mutual converse with Nature".

Algernon Swinburne (1837-1909) has described this *hen kai pan* recently in more appropriate language in his poem *Hertha*. Thus a metaphysical need as Schopenhauer called it, has again and again called forth poems and semi-philosophical ideal poems (F A Lange) of the All-One. Western thinkers, for example, Schelling have, however, attempted to convey the teaching of Universal Oneness more convincingly through the medium of an unfortunate philosophy of identity and more recently through an even less convincing form of Monism. In his *Darstellung meines Systems der Philosophie* (1801) Schelling wished to prove that the perceptive consciousness and its object, Nature, were one. Time conditioned poetical moods are possible from a oneness outwards, but not judgment of thoughts which are timelessly valid. Any thinker, who wishes to prove in a comprehensible manner that material and spirit or body and soul, or thinking and Being, or subject and object, are One and the same, or identical, overlooks the fact that such terms as material or power or spirit or Being already correspond to the judgments of a discerning subject, which faces an object — Rückert's "object of knowledge", even if this object is one's own body or the personal spiritual stimulation of the thinker.

How can the One or the Universal or the All-One, which according to their nature are indissolubly one, be split into two, namely into a perceiving subject and an object of perception? How can they so be arranged that they become released from themselves in such a way that, thinking themselves in opposition to each other, they understand each other and name themselves accordingly? Nevertheless poets and enthusiastic poetic thinkers of the Indo-European peoples have again and again been compelled to express by unnatural imagery, what cannot be imparted in comprehensible language as a generally valid judgment. In this light we must examine the different kinds of Pantheism and Mysticism, as also Goethe's "Godnature", an Indo-European exposition of Spinoza's *Deus sive natura*, which resulted from Spinoza incorporating Indo-European ideas from the Stoics and the Pantheist Giordano Bruno.

Any thinker who wishes to equate God, the world and human spiritual life as one, such as is attempted by some poets at inspired moments, will in the Indo-European domain be confronted by destiny — as has been shown above, an all too difficult object of perception to be redeemed in a becalming or inspiring Universal-Oneness.

How was it possible, that belief in a God and Gods among the Indo-European peoples became transmitted, first with the Indians, then with the other peoples, and finally also with the Islamised and Christianised peoples, into Pantheism and mysticism?

Hildebrecbt Hommel[39] has shown that the figure of a heavenly father originally common to all Indo-Europeans — known by the Indians as *Djaus pitar*, by the Hellenes as *Zeus Pater*, and by the Romans as *Jupiter* (from *Diupater*) — was elevated above the other Gods at an early point in time and recognised as a god of the Universe by the Teutons, as the Icelander Snorri proves — the "All Father" (in Old Nordic, *alfadir*), which Indo-European mysticism later discovered in the soul of the religious man. In upper Bavaria and in Tyrol the description Heavenly Father has been preserved amongst the farmers and transferred to the Christian God — an orderer and protector of a universe without beginning and end, and hence, as the Hellenes said, a "Father of Gods and Men", in the Christian God, the creator of a universe with a beginning in time. The transition from the father of the heavens, a term which possibly belongs to the Bronze Age, to an inner worldly and spiritual

God, was gradually accomplished by the Indo-Europeans towards the end of their early period, which was full of Sagas of the Gods. In India this transition took place from the ninth century BC onwards in the Upanishads, in which the world was not seen as the creation of a God: the universe was a timeless essence, the *brahman*, which dwells in all things and all souls. Paul Deussen (*Vedanta und Platonismus im Lichte der Kantischen Philosophie*, Comenius-Schriften zur Geistesgeschichte, Zweites Heft, 1922, pp 19-20) — has shown that, even in the most recent songs of the Rigvedas, the existence of the traditional Indo-aryan world of the Gods is doubted, and that even here — as later in Hellas — philosophic thought forced its way through as a premonition or certainty of the unity of all existence. In the Rigveda (1,164) it is said: "What is the One, poets call manifold" (K F Geldner: *Der RigVeda aus dem Sanskrit ins Deutsche Übersetzt*, Erster Teil, 1951, p 236). The simple men of remote agricultural communities did not participate readily in this transition from the manifold Gods of the universe to a sole God. The isolated Italic farmers still worshipped and celebrated their native Gods in festivals, the *di indigentes* of the early Roman period, when in the capital, Rome, after the Olympic Gods of the Hellenes had been equated to the ancient Roman divinities (*numina*), an inner-worldly deity had already been anticipated and conceived by thinking men. The general Indo-European transition from the Gods of the Sagas to Pantheism and Mysticism, which took place amongst those who by choice or by force were converted to Christianity or Islam, despite the resistance of true believers, can be briefly portrayed as follows.

After their early period and in the middle age of their development — on the way "from myth to Logos" (W Nestle) — the Bronze Age idea of the Gods and God gradually grew dim among logical and resolutely thinking men in the Indo-European peoples, whose hereditary dispositions directed them towards reason. This school of free thought recognised that it was childish to imagine that the Gods lived somewhere out in space, reaching down into the human world, and these ideas necessarily carried less and less conviction to thinking men, when they became convinced that the gods too were governed by destiny. Thus there gradually evolved the idea of an inner-worldly and inner-spiritual deity (Pantheism) and of a God working within us (Mysticism) — the *dominans ille in nobis deus*, as Marcus Tullius Cicero (*Tusculanae disputationes* 1, 74) called this divinity. Thus Pantheism was joined by rational mysticism, perception and inner experience, which postulates that the individual immersing himself in himself experiences self-comprehension in its ultimate form as the universal soul, and concludes that the *atman*, or individual soul, is, in the final analysis a part of *brahman*, as the Indians described such mysticism.

The pantheistic width of vision and mystical inner contemplation of the Indo-Europeans (compare p64) were interchangeable — if not in comprehensible thought, at least in poetical moods. The power pervading the universe and the power felt by the soul as it sank into the universal soul could be felt to flow together in one. In the first years of his stay at Weimar, Goethe happily agreed with a sentence which he found in Cicero's *de Divinatione* (I, 49): everything is filled by divine spirit and hence the souls of men are moved by communion with the divine souls (*cumque omnia complete et referta sint aeterno sensu et mente divina, necesse est contagione divinorum animorum animos humanos commoveri*). This again is the premonition of a deity which expresses the divine in the universe as the basis of the soul.

The fearless thinkers among the Teutons, above all among the North Teutons, to whom the world of the Gods of the Asas and Vanir had become a childish idea, must have recognised long before the penetration of Christianity the existence of an inner-worldly and inner-spiritual deity, a *brahman*, or a *theion*, as the Hellenes called it, a *daimonion*, such as Socrates felt working within himself. It is a striking fact, to which too little attention has been paid hitherto, that the word "God" was neuter in gender in the Teutonic languages (*Das Gott*, or, in Old Nordic *gud*) and that it was only after the false interpretation by Christian converters that the word acquired male gender. Thus thinking Indians no longer spoke of Gods even at an early period, but of a deity governing the world (*dewata*), which was also called the brahman. This is the *deus in nobis* of Hellenic and Roman poets and thinkers. When Christian missionaries asked the north Teutons who or what they believed in, they received the reply which centuries previously the south Teutons (who had believed in *Das Gott* (neuter) might also have given that they believed in their power (*matt*) or strength (*magin*), a power working within them, a deity filling the religious man, an inner-worldly and inner-spiritual deity. Such an answer must have seemed to the missionaries, as it would to many present-day commentators, a mere boast of power or an idolatrous presumption, while in fact it must be understood as a factual "The God" (*Das Gott*) corresponding to the *dominans ille in nobis deus*. But it is easy to understand that the missionaries, who in Christianity had accepted the extramundane, transcendent ideas of a "personal" God, from the Semitic peoples, were at a loss when confronted by faith in a destiny ruling within men.

The pagan north Germans, who still believed that the divine was present in all "men of high mind", were called Godless (*gudlauss* or *gudlausir menn*) by their converted countrymen, who were spiritually more simple, and therefore could not understand inner spiritual power or strength.

The men with more insight among the Hellenes would have understood the neuter God — *Das Gott* — of the Teutons, for it corresponded to their own "*to theion*". Thinking Hellenes had already long replaced the plurality of the Gods by the single deity and later by the single figure called The Mighty (*to Kreitton*). The orator Dion of Prusa, known as Chrysostom (40-120), and the philosopher Plotinus (approx. 204-270), would not have misunderstood the Icelanders: Might and Power as descriptions of the deity were familiar to them. Dion of Prusa (XXXI, 11) says of the deeply prudent men of his time: "They simply combine all Gods together in one might (*ischys*) and power (*dynamis*) " and Plotinus expresses this in the *Enneads* (1, 6, 8) in the same way as Goethe, who read this passage in the year 1805:

> *Läg' nicht in uns des Gottes eigne Kraft,*
> *wie könnt' uns Göttliches entzücken?*

If the Gods own power did not lie within us,
how could the divine enrapture us?

(*Zahme Xenien* III, 725, 26.)

The might or power of which the Indo-Europeans had a presentiment, this unity of the deity was split up by thinkers in the realm of human experience into the trinity of "The Good, the True and the Beautiful", but in such a way that these ideas or words remained close neighbours in Hellas. Here and there with the later Hellenic-Roman thinkers the true could easily be understood as the good and the beautiful, *aletheia* could signify both intellectual truth as well as moral truth, and in the *kalok'agathia* the ideal of sifting and selection, of *eugeneia* or human disciplined choice, bodily beauty and moral fitness, and virtue (*arete*) became linked with one another. Since Plato's *Banquet*, Indo-European thinkers have recognised truth, beauty and virtue as life values which pointed beyond the realm of experience to the divine, to the *brahman*, or the concept of *Das Gott* (neuter) — to a deity which through truth rendered the thinking man capable of knowledge.

The reappearance of Indo-European religious attitudes, also explains why Christian theologians as well as thinkers and poets of the Christianised west again and again revolted against the concepts of an other-worldly, personal God — of a God who had created the world from nothing and had populated it with creatures according to his design. The French mystic and scholar, Amalrich of Bena, who died in Paris about 1206, was even cursed after his death by the Church because he rationally rejected the teachings of God as a creator, and because he had asserted that such a God must be responsible for the sorrow of all living creatures and for the vices of man, since he had created them all. Amalrich, the Pantheistic mystic, knew as a result of his Indo-European disposition, that the justification (*Theodicy*) by the all-powerful, all knowing, and all-merciful God, of the evils of his creation, was impossible.

The outlook of Amalrich of Bena, however, had already been expressed in north India after it had been penetrated by Indo-European migrants in the pre-Christian centuries and especially by Samkhya teaching, by Jains and Buddhists, who guarded themselves against non-Indo-European theistic religions infiltrating from Southern India: God the creator must be reproached with having either created or permitted the existence of liars, thieves and murderers.

The Indo-European concept of destiny relieved the Gods from responsibility for the evil of earthly life, and Epicurus, who himself no longer believed in Gods (cf. Eduard Schwartz: *Charakterköpfe aus der Antike*, 1943, p147; Epicurus: *Philosophie der Freude*, translated by Johannes Mewaldt, 1956), advised his contemporaries who did, to imagine them as creatures, who lived a blessed, untroubled life amongst the stars without bothering about men, neither using nor harming them. Such an idea had already appeared in the *Iliad* (XXIV, 525) centuries before Epicurus. There Achilles attempts to console Priamos bowed down by sorrow, with the words:

Thus have the Gods determined it for the wretched men,
To live sorrowfully, but they themselves are struck by no sorrow.

Shakespeare (*King Lear*, IV, 1) puts the same embittered thoughts on Gloucester's lips:

As flies to wanton boys are we to the Gods —
They kill us for their sport.

This idea was adopted by Hölderlin in *Hyperion's Song of Destiny* and by Tennyson in his poem *The Lotus Eaters*. Kant, in his *Critique of the Power of Judgment* (Part II, p 85), defended the Hellenes and Romans in these words: "One cannot count it so highly to their blame, if they conceived their Gods... as limited, for when they studied the artifices and course of Nature, they encountered the good and evil, the purposeful and pointless in it... and only with the greatest difficulty could they have formed a different judgment of its cause".

Theodicies were not necessary for the Indo-Europeans, because over the Gods stood merciless destiny. (Virgil: *inexorabile fatum*). Within Christianity however, Pantheism and Mysticism again and again sought to set themselves against the church's teachings of an all powerful, all-knowing, predestined and yet all-good creator. The church answered with condemnation and burning; examples are numerous: Origen, Scotus Erigenus, Hugo of St Victor, Amalrich of Bena, David of Dinant, Meister Eckhart, Nicolaus von Kues, Sebastian Frank, Miguel Servedo (Servet), Vanini, Valentin Weigel, Jakob Böhme, Angelus Silesius, Fénéelon, Herder, Fichte, Schelling, Schleiermacher, Shelley, Tegner, Kuno Fischer and others.

Thus the religiosity of the Indo-Europeans, which appears whenever their nature can unfold itself freely, emerges only in that form which religious science has described as nature religions. Here however, it may be said, that Indo-European religiosity in the West has also been repeatedly misinterpreted and misunderstood, for the outlook is widespread that the more the faith, all the greater the religiosity, which is to be found where men feel drawn to "supernatural" values. In a far more inward sense than the description nature religion commonly implies, the belief and religiosity of the Indo-Europeans represent the natural, balanced conduct of the worshipping mind, and the heroic power of thought as it is found in the honest Nordic man. Powerful spontaneous thought and ordered worship of the deity here strengthen and deepen one another. The more richly a man cultivates these facilities the more perfect in his humanness, the more truly religious does he become at the same time.

No pressing forward to God is possible in this attitude of mind and spirit, no rigid belief, no pretence of a duty to believe, no anxiety to please the deity; freedom and dignity and the composure of the noble spirited, even under deep stress, are characteristic of the purest religiosity. Indeed, one can almost say that Indo-European religiosity and morality (in contrast to the commands and penalties of a God who promises reward and punishment) emanates from the dignity of man, the dignity of *humanitas* — from a *dignitas* which is characteristic of the great-minded and well-born. According to Cicero, a great and strong-minded person (*fortis animus et magnus*) wishes to carry himself with honour (*Honestum: de officiis*, I, 72-73, 94-95, 101, 106, 130; III, 23-24) because in such conduct reason controls desire. Thus the Roman concept of *humanitas* as interpreted above, presupposes "the centuries long breeding of an aristocratic type of man" (Franz Beckmann: *Humanitas, Ursprung und Idee*, 1952, p 7). Hence Hellenic-Roman *humanitas* cannot become a morality for everyone; in Hellas it was the morality of the *eleutheroi*, in Rome that of the *ingenui*, or of the free-born, and it could not be transferred to the freedmen (*liberti*). In the Middle Ages the church used the word *humanitas* to describe human lowliness (*humilitas*) when faced by the extra-mundial, other worldly God. It was not until the advent of the scholars of the Renaissance in Florence, around 1400 AD, that *humanitas* was again understood to mean human dignity, and conceived of as a duty which it was incumbent on man to observe.

When today praise is lavished on so-called works of art, it is almost tragic to recall that Friedrich Schiller demanded this very *humanitas* and *dignitas* above all from artists; just as Marcus Tullius Cicero did of the Italici:

> The dignity of man is given into your hands
> Preserve it !
> It falls with you, it will rise with you.

As far as the mature religiosity of the Indo-Europeans is concerned, their morality does not, like the morality of the Bible, spring from a commandment of God, from a "Thou shalt not!" (3 Moses xix 18; Matthew v. 43; Luke vi. 27). Indo-European morality springs from the positive dignity of the high-minded man, to whom humanity or human love, which may best be described as good-will, comes as second nature — *maitri* in Sanscrit, or *metta* in Pali, or *eumeneia*, *philanthropia* or *sympatheia* in Greek, or *benevolentia* or *comitas* in Latin. Biblical morality is of alien law (*heteronom*). Indo-European morality is of its own law (*autonom*). Compared with the biblical admonition to love thy neighbour (*agape*), which originally only applied to the fellow members of the tribe, the concept of good-will is perhaps more valid, since love cannot be commanded.

Burkhard Wilhelm Leist (*Alt-arisches Jus gentium*, 1889, p 173; *ibid, Alt-arisches Jus civile*, 1892-96, 228, 241, 381-82; 1892 [Vol. 1, p21]) has proved that such humanity and good will already existed in the oldest legal records of the Indo-Europeans, that Indo-European human dignity had demanded that in man one should always see one's fellow and meet him with *acquitas*, or good will (*maitri, metta*), one of the highest values of ancient India, and above all of Buddhist morality. According to the *Odyssey*, (VI, 207; VII, 165; IX, 270) Zeus himself guides the worthy man who implores him for help and avenges strangers who are cast out and those in need of protection: *Zeus xenios*, who looks after strangers and all those in want, corresponds to the *dii hospitales* of the Romans. The Edda advises in the "Teachings to Loddfafnir" (21, 23):

> Never show
> Scorn and mockery
> To the stranger and traveller!
> Never scold the stranger,
> Never drive him away from the gate!
> Be helpful to the hungering!
>
> (*Edda*, Vol. 11, 1920 translated from
> the German of Felix Genzmer, pp. 137, 138).

However, to the Teutons, who according to Tacitus (*Germania* XXI) were the most hospitable of all peoples, "moral demands were not divine commands", for them a good deed had no reward, an evil deed expected no punishment by the deity (Hans Kuhn, *Sitte und Sittlichkeit, in Germanische Altertumskunde*, edited by Hermann Schneider, 1938, p 177). Man's attempt to wheedle himself into favour with the Gods by offering sacrifices is censured by the *Edda* (Havamal 145):

> Better not to have implored for anything,
> than to have sacrificed too much;
> the gift looks for reward.

The morality of human dignity is not inspired on account of the prospect of a reward in heaven, but for its own sake: *nihil praeter id quod honestum sit propter se esse expetendum.* This was how Cicero understood the Roman religiosity and morality (*de Officiis* 1, 72-75, 94-95, 106, 130; ibid, III, 23-24, 33; *Tusculanae disputationes* V, 1), which both originate from ancient Italic and hence Indo-European nature. Such aims as the Hellenic *kalok'agathia* (beauty and fitness), and that of the Roman *humanitas* — *humanitas* being understood in the era of the Roman aristocratic republic as a duty or ideal of full manhood, of human wholeness, or of Noble nature[40] — such goals of heroic perfection are therefore particularly expressive of Indo-European religiosity which offers the worship of a resolute, heroic heart.

It can be shown, and could be proved in detail, that in Europe and North America, the noblest men and women, even those who admitted to accepting a church belief handed down to them, behaved and spoke in the decisive hours of their lives according to the religious disposition, actions and morality of the Indo-European.

Indo-European spiritual history had commenced at the beginning of the first pre-Christian millennium with outstanding works like the Vedas (cf. KF Geldner, *Vedismus und Brahmanismus*, Religionsgeschichtliches Lesebuch, Vol. IX, 1928) and the Upanishads, which Schopenhauer (*Parerga und Paralipomena*, Chapter XVI) called not only the "consolation of his life", but also the "consolation of his death". The Indo-Europeans entered the stage of world history with Kurasch (Cyros) II, the Persian king of the Hakamanish family of the Achaeminides, who ruled from 559 to 529 BC, and founded the great Persian kingdom which extended from India to Egypt (cf. Albert T Olmstead: *A History of the Persian Empire*, 1948, p 34 *et seq*) The Hellenic historian Xenophon wrote about Kurash the Great in his *Kyrupaideia*. The Persians under the Achaemenides, with the Hellenes, "brothers and sisters of the same blood" (Aeschylus, *The Persians*, Verse 185), are described by Bundahishn (XIV), a Persian saga book of the ninth century (G Widengren, *Iranische Geisteswelt*, 1961, p 75) as "fair and radiant eyed". According to Herodotus (1,136) they taught their sons "to ride, to shoot, with the bow and to speak the truth". The religion of Mazdaism regarded lies and deceit (German: *Trug*, Persian *drug*) as a basic evil, truth as a basic virtue.

Since the advent of the twentieth century the Indo-Europeans have begun to withdraw from the spiritual history of the world. Particularly today, what is described as most "progressive" in music, the plastic arts and literature of the "free west" is already no longer Indo-European in spirit.

CHAPTER SEVEN

THE greatest ideas of mankind have been conceived in the lands between India and Germania, between Iceland and Benares (where Buddha began to teach) amongst the peoples of Indo-European language; and these ideas have been accompanied by the Indo-European religious attitude which represents the highest attainments of the mature spirit. When in January 1804, in conversation with his colleague, the philologist Riemer, Goethe expressed the view that he found it "remarkable that the whole of Christianity had not brought forth a Sophocles", his knowledge of comparative religion was restricted by the knowledge of his age, yet he had unerringly chosen as the precursor of an Indo-European religion the poet Sophocles, "typical of the devout Athenian ... in his highest, most inspired form",[41] a poet who represented the religiosity of the people before the people (*demos*) of Athens had degenerated into a mass (*ochlos*). But where apart from the Indo-Europeans, has the world produced a more devout man with such a great soul as the Athenian, Sophodes?

Where outside the Indo-European domain have religions arisen, which have combined such greatness of soul with such high flights of reason (*logos, ratio*) and such wide vision (*theoria*)? Where have religious men achieved the same spiritual heights as Spitama Zarathustra, as the teachers of the Upanishads, as Homer, as Buddha and even as Lucretius Carus, Wilhelm von Humboldt and Shelley?

Goethe wished that Homer's songs might become our Bible. Even before the discovery of the spiritual heights and power of the pre-Christian Teuton but especially after Lessing, Winckelmann and Heinrich Voss, the translator of Homer, the Indo-European

81

outlook renewed itself in Germany, recalling a world of the spirit which was perfected by great German poets and thinkers during the late eighteenth and early nineteenth centuries.

Since Goethe's death (1832), and since the death of Wilhelm von Humboldt (1835), the translator of the devout Indo-European *Bhagavadgita*, this Indo-European spirit, which also revealed itself in the pre-Christian Teuton, has vanished.

Goethe had a premonition of this decline of the West: even in October 1801 he remarked in conversation with the Countess von Egloffstein, that spiritual emptiness and lack of character were spreading — as if he had foreseen what today characterises the most celebrated literature of the Free West. It may be that Goethe had even foreseen, in the distant future, the coming of an age in which writers would make great profits by the portrayal of sex and crime for the masses. As Goethe said to Eckermann, on 14th March 1830, "the representation of noble bearing and action is beginning to be regarded as boring, and efforts are being made to portray all kinds of infamies". Previously in a letter to Schiller of 9th August 1797, he had pointed out at least one of the causes of the decline: in the larger cities men lived in a constant frenzy of acquisition and consumption and had therefore become incapable of the very mood from which spiritual life arises. Even then he was tortured and made anxious, although he could observe only the beginnings of the trend, the sight of the machine system gaining the upper hand; he foresaw that it would come and strike (*Willhelm Meisters Wanderjahre*, Third Book, Chapter 15, Cotta's jubilee edition, Vol. XX, p 190). In a letter to his old friend Zelter, on 6th June 1825, he pronounced it as his view that the educated world remained rooted in mediocrity, and that a century had begun "for competent heads, for practical men with an easy grasp of things, who... felt their superiority above the crowd, even if they themselves are not talented enough for the highest achievements"; pure simplicity was no longer to be found, although there was a sufficiency of simple stuff; young men would be excited too early and then torn away by the vortex of the time. Therefore Goethe exhorted youth in his poem *Legacy* of the year 1829:

Join yourself to the smallest host!

In increasing degree since approximately the middle of the nineteenth century poets and writers as well as journalists — the descendants of the "competent heads" by whom Goethe was alarmed even in the year 1801 — have made a virtue out of necessity by representing characterlessness as a fact. With Thomas Mann this heartless characterlessness first gained world renown. Mann used his talent to conceal his spiritual desolation by artifices which have been proclaimed by contemporary admirers as insurpassable. But the talent of the writers emulating Thomas Mann no longer sufficed even to conceal their spiritual emptiness, although many of their readers, themselves spiritually impoverished, have not noticed this.

The freedom of the Press, which was introduced through the constitution of May 1816 into the Duchy of Weimar and which had already been demanded by Wieland with his superficial judgment would, Goethe, declared, do nothing more than give free rein to authors with a deep contempt of public opinion, (Zahme Xenien: *Goethes Sämtliche Werke*, Cotta's Jubilee edition, Vol. IV, p 47; *Annalen* (Annals) 1816, same edition, Vol. XXX, p 298). In the *Annalen* of 1816, he remarked that every right-thinking man of learning in the world foresaw the direct and incalculable consequences of this act with fright and regret. Thus even in his time, Goethe must have reflected how little the men of the Press, were capable of combining freedom with human dignity.

When the descendants of the competent heads of the beginning of the nineteenth century rose, through their talents, to the upper classes, where due to a lower birthrate their families finally died out, the eliminating process of social climbing in Europe seized hold of less capable heads and bore them away into the vortex of the time. Their culture has been described most mercilessly by Friedrich Nietzsche in his lectures of the year 1871-72: "*Concerning the future of our educational institutions*" (Pocket edition, Vol. 1, 1906, pp 314, 332-333, 396). Nietzscbe above all concentrated on famous contemporary writers, "the hasty and vain production, the despicable manufacturing of books, the perfected lack of style, the shapelessness and characterlessness or the lamentable dilution of their expressions, the loss of every aesthetic canon, the lust for anarchy and chaos" — which he described as if he had actually seen the most celebrated literature of the Free West, whose known authors no longer mastered their own languages even to the extent still demanded by popular school teachers around 1900. These vociferous heralds of the need for culture in an era of general education were rejected by Nietzsche who in this displayed true IndoEuropean views — as fanatical opponents of the true culture, which holds firm to the aristocratic nature of the spirit. If Nietzsche described the task of the West as to find the culture appropriate to Beethoven, then the serious observer today will recognise only too well the situation which Nietzsche foresaw and described as a laughing stock and a thing of shame.

In the year 1797, Friedrich Schiller composed a poem *Deutsche Grösse*. Full of confidence in the German spirit he expressed the view that defeat in war by stronger foes could not touch German dignity which was a great moral force. The precious possession of the German language would also be preserved. Schiller (*Das Siegesfest*) certainly knew what peoples had to expect of war:

> For Patrocles lies buried
> and Thersites comes back

but he must have imagined that the losses of the best in the fight could be replaced. The dying-out of families of dignity and moral stature, (*megalopsychia* and *magnanimitas*), had then not yet begun in Europe.

In the year 1929, just a decade after the First World War had ended, that Peloponnesian war of the Teutonic peoples, which caused both in England and in Germany excessively heavy losses of gifted young men, of officers and aristocrats, Oskar Walzel (*Die Geistesströmungen des 19. Jahrhunderts*, 1929, p 43), Professor of German literature at the university of Bonn, gave it as his opinion that after this war the trend to de-spiritualise Germany had gained ground far more rapidly than hitherto: "Is there in German history in general such an identical want of depth in men to be observed as at present?" But for the Germans it is poor consolation that this 'de-spiritualising' is just as marked in other Western countries. Another sign of this trend is that today many famous writers are no longer capable of preserving the precious possession of the German language. Other Western languages are also neglecting their form and literature, but this again is poor consolation for the Germans. Such neglect is considered by many writers today as characteristic of, and part of the process of gaining their freedom and liberation from all traditional outlook. Goethe criticised this as a false idea of freedom (Maxims and Reflections, *Goethes sämtliche Werke*, Cottas Jubilaumsausgabe, Bd. IV, p 229) in the following words:

"Everything which liberates our spirit, without increasing our mastery of ourselves, is pernicious." Thus, by freedom Goethe also understood the dignity of the freeborn, not the nature and mode of life of the freed slave.

CHAPTER EIGHT

Q UINTUS Horatius Flaccus (*Carmina* III, pp. 25, 27) has described the task of all art, especially of poetry, as being to create "nothing small and in a low manner" (*nil parvum aut humili modo*). Yet the most popular literature of the free West, and the culture of mass media, today emphasises the unimportant sexual experiences of unbridled men, often in a degrading and unclean manner, and this is described by many newspaper critics as "art". The churches also patronise such forms of art for the masses and attempt to secure the attendance of youth by offering religious jazz and Negro rhythms. The best examples of pure sexual experience, as accomplished in the *nil parvutn aut humili modo* of Horace, may be found in the truly Indo-European Homer. According to C F von Nigelsbach (*Homerische Theologie*, third edition, edited by G. Authenrieth, 1884, p 229) Homer always represented sensuality without lust and without prudery and never enticingly and seductively or with sensual excitement in mind; he was one of the most innocent poets of all ages and even in describing sexual scenes, he never used a word which exceeded artistic requirements. This is yet another example of how the Indo-European linked freedom with dignity.

In Europe and North America, individuals who were still capable of their own religiosity — of which the *Commonplace Book* of Thomas Jefferson, the distinguished third President of the United States of America, is an example — have been replaced by masses who by religiosity only understand an appendage to a confession useful for personal advancement. There is no possible hope, under these circumstances, that the great spiritual and religious heights

87

which were reached by the Indo-Europeans living between Europe
and India at various times from the Bronze Age up to the nineteenth century will ever be matched again. For a world culture
such as 'progressives' seek to construct, an elevation of the spirit
above and beyond the entertainment needs of the masses — above
jazz and Negro rhythm — is no longer to be hoped for, since what
Europeans and North Americans have to offer today to the "undeveloped" peoples (who, however, should have been able to utilise
the 10,000 to 20,000 years which have passed since the end of the
Old Stone Age for their own development) is nothing more than
the spiritually vacuous "culture" of a welfare state governed by a
hundred soulless authorities. In such societies the press, literature,
radio, television and films and other media provide the masses
with a controlled "tensioning" and "de-tensioning" by alternately
playing up this or that belief or unbelief. With the further extinction
of families capable of spiritual independence, and the further disappearance of talents[42] particularly amongst the peoples of North
America and Europe capable of spiritual leadership, no alternative
to the disappearance of the last remaining elements of the Indo-
European peoples and their culture can be expected.

Thomas Jefferson (1743-1826), one of the founders of the free
state of Virginia, author of the *Declaration of Independence* (1776),
Governor of Virginia, ambassador in Paris, Foreign Minister under
George Washington, and from 1801 to 1809 President of the United
States, sought to see his people as a nation of Teutonic yeomen
and distrusted trade and the upcoming industry of the cities, which
he regarded as foes of freedom. Jefferson sought to protect the
freedom and dignity of the individual man from the state, to which
he therefore wished to allow only a minimum of power. To preserve this farmer aristocracy enjoying Indo-European freedom[43]
he sought to avoid a centralised state in favour of a loose federation
or association of the former English colonies. But after the agricultural era, the urbanisation and industrialisation of the industrial
era brought into being the city masses whose need for security
became greater than their real or pretended urge to freedom.
Security against (in the Indo-European sense) destiny — cowardly

security against all difficult situations of life — can only be achieved in a state based upon bureaucracy, a state which is therefore, of necessity, inhuman. The excessive number of patronising departments and repressive laws, as well as the large number of officials in dependent positions, gradually stifles the freedom of any individuals still capable of a dignified and courageous conduct of life. (Tacitus, *Annals* XXXVII: *corruptissima in re publica plurimae leges.*)

In the winter of 1791-92, Wilhelm von Humboldt, the friend of Schiller, and like Schiller one of the last great Indo-Europeans, wrote a book: *Ideen zu einem Versuch, die Grenzen der Wirksamkeit des Staates zu bestimmen.* (An attempt to determine the limits of the effectiveness of the State). In this work he sought to safeguard the *humanitas* and *dignitas*, the dignity of man, from patronisation by governmental welfare states. Yet with the twentieth century, more and more countries, including the once-so-free English, and now in their wake, North America, have become "socialised", bureaucratic welfare states, whose masses, encumbered by thousands of officials and organisations, have begun to forget freedom and dignity through the de-tensioning offered them. With the loss of freedom and dignity in political and social life, how is the preservation of traditional spiritual values possible?

One of the first to recognise that the era of the free individual, capable of self-determination, was coming to an end, and that with the displacement of this free, self-reliant man, human dignity would vanish from public life, was the Norman Count Alexis de Tocqueville (1805-1859), the friend of Count Arthur Cobineau (1816-1882). His work *L'Ancien Régime et la Revolution* (7th edition 1866) and the *Souvenirs de A de Tocqueville* (1893), which were not published until thirty-four years after the death of the author, were only heeded in Germany when it was too late to save the freedom of the individual; de Tocqueville studied the nature of the democracies as displayed in their land of origin, in North America, and afterwards wrote his work *De la Démocratie en Amérique* (1835), a warm-hearted and richly informative description of the North American free state, in which he also warned of the dangers facing democracies which fell under the domination of the spirit of the masses. He feared that the rise of an era of the masses, with state capitalism and state-controlled enterprise, would pervert the democracies into repressing the freedom of the individual man of dignity — to him the highest human good — so that democracy would lead to a suppression of freedom in the Indo-European sense, the freedom still demanded by Jefferson and by Wilhelm von Humboldt.

The last men who — without investigating its origins — defended Indo-European freedom, namely the democracy of the free and mutually-equal land-owning family fathers, were the English philosophers John Stuart Mill (Michael St. John Packe, *The Life of John Stuart Mill*, 1954, pp 488 *et seq.*) and Herbert Spencer. JS Mill wrote a book *On Liberty* in 1859. With almost incomprehensible farsightedness Mill recognised the threat to the dignity and freedom of independent and self-reliant individual thinking men which was embodied in the "freedom" of the masses gathering in the cities. Mill feared the tyranny of the majorities in the popular assemblies, the repression of those capable of judgment by the mass of alternating public opinions. He feared the Chinese ideal of the sameness of all men and saw — like Goethe in his tragedy *Die natürliche Tochter* (I. 5) — that all contemporary political trends were aiming to reshape the era by raising the depths, and debasing the heights. When men had been made "equal" by law, every deviation from this uniformity would be condemned as wicked, immoral, monstrous and unnatural (John Stuart Mill, *Die Freiheit*, 1859 translated into German by Elsa Wentscher, *Philosophische Bibliothek*, Vol. CCII, 1928, pp. 7, 100 *et seq.*). Hence in the year 1859, when England was still free, that very conformity was already predicted against which even the newspaper writers and literateurs of unhindered mass circulation today complain.

To John Stuart Mill the freedom of the individual was the highest good. He started with the viewpoint of Adam Smith and David Ricardo and inclined to socialism, but feared that the abuse of freedom by parties and majorities would lead to the rule of the masses, to the end of competition and to the abolition of individual possessions, which would favour the stupid and lazy, but rob the clever and industrious. For this reason Mill also advocated Malthusianism and family planning, because families with many children whom they were economically incapable of supporting would endanger the state.

Herbert Spencer found the highest degree of freedom within the state in England in the middle nineteenth century, the highest degree of freedom for men of independent judgment and independent conscience. But when he wrote his *Principles of Sociology* in 1896, he recognized that this freedom was already threatened by socialism. Socialism he said, would appear in every industrial society and would repress every freedom; socialism itself would become only another form of subjection, simply another form of the bureaucratic regime, and thus it would become the greatest misfortune that the world had ever experienced; no one might ever again do what he pleased, each would have to do what he was ordered to do. A total and absolute loss of freedom would result. Herbert Spencer might have added that only a minority of men capable of independent thought would regret the loss of freedom in a bureaucratic, patronising state, while the solid majority (Ibsen: *An Enemy of the People*) would prefer state care to freedom, being unable to understand the freedom of Jefferson or Wilhelm von Humboldt, or Mill or Spencer (Herbert Spencer, *Principles of Sociology*, Vol. III, 1897, pp 585, 595).

In two contributions to his Essays (*Essays: Scientific, Political and Speculative*, Vol. II, 1883, pp 48, 56, 66, 94, 100, 104; Vol. III, 1878, pp 181, 186) Herbert Spencer the Liberal summarised how socialism — when it finally penetrated all parties — would repress the freedom of the individual to voice independent judgment; through a flood of laws there would arise, supported by the blind faith of the socialist masses in enactments, and in government machinery, a stupid and ponderous bureaucratic state; the state would discourage its citizens from helping themselves, and no one would be permitted to withdraw from the national institutions, as they may from private ones, when they broke down or became too costly; the blind belief in officialdom, above all in the Fascist and National-Socialist form, has given rise, as Spencer feared, to a blind faith in government, to a political fetishism. But wherever socialist governments have been able to rule uncontested for decades, officialdom, state control and state fetishism have set in, and with them a further repression of the freedom of the individual, of that Indo-European and above all Teutonic freedom emanating from the spirit of the landowning family heads, equal among one another, with which Spencer and the liberals of his day were concerned even though they did not realise that the roots of this freedom were historically Indo-European.

One may describe the Teutons as born democrats, if by democracy one understands the self-conscious freedom and equality of rural yeomen. Democracy of this kind will always follow the command, found in the Edda (*Grogaldr VI: Der Zaubergesang der Groa, Edda*, Vol. II, 1920, P 178): "Lead thyself!" This freedom, a dignified freedom found only in the man capable of self-determination, was maintained in Iceland, whence Norwegian freeholders removed themselves to avoid forcible conversion to Christianity at the hands of the newly-converted Norwegian kings, with such resolution, that the present day observer must doubt whether the Icelandic free state could in general be called a state.

Likewise Eduard Meyer, (*Geschichte des Altertums*, Vol. I, II, 1909, p. 777) has alluded to the individualism and self-determination which characterises the Indo-Europeans, to the individuality of the self-determining man, hostile to every kind of leadership, even to the extent of frequently proving a danger to his own nation or state. Bismarck himself bore witness to this individuality when he said that he was less concerned with giving commands than with punishing disobedience. Such an outlook is expressed in the motto, valid earlier in Germany, *Selbst ist der Mann* — Rely on yourself — and this outlook refuses charity from every other, even from the state. It corresponds to a truly Indo-European remark of the Emperor Marcus Aurelius Antoninus (*Observations*, 111, 5): "You shall stand upright, and not be supported by others! " In the *Agamemnon* (755) of Aeschylus, the king of the Hellenic army, first among equals, expresses the view that he has his own convictions, apart from those of his people. With Sophocles (*Aias*, 481) the

Chorus confirms to Aias, who has freely chosen death, that he never spoke a word which did not proceed directly from his own nature.

But such attitudes have tended to disappear lately amongst Indo-European speaking peoples — corresponding to the disappearance of men capable of independent thought and opinion, the truly free-born. Recently, through an accumulation of men incapable of independent thought, city masses have come into existence which wish to be led: it is no longer "lead yourself — yourself!" but "Leader, command and we will follow!" In such periods true Indo-European freedom vanishes. Marcus Tullius Cicero (*de officio*, 1, 112-13), imbued with the traditional freedom of an aristocratic republic and acquainted through Panactius with the Hellenic thinkers' doctrines of freedom, still risked praising Julius Caesar's dead opponent Cato Uticensis, during the former's dictatorship. After the battle of Thapsos, many Romans accepted the sole rule of a conquering leader of the city masses (consisting predominantly of freedmen), the *dictator perpetuus*, Julius Caesar. Not, however, Cato Uticensis, one of the last freeborn men of the aristocratic Roman republic: Cato's love of freedom taught him to choose death rather than live under tyranny.

The historical work of Tacitus, which has already been mentioned above, reveals that Indo-European freedom (*libertas*) is only possible in a society of individuals capable of independent judgment, who rely on their own resources and who do not need to be supported. Herbert Spencer had already seen, towards the end of the nineteenth century, that such freedom would no longer be practicable in industrial societies.

Indo-European spiritual freedom and human dignity have been represented with the utmost beauty by the classical art of the Hellenes and this spirit speaks with irrepressible vigour and clarity from the sculptures which represent Hellenic thinkers and poets (K. Schefeld, *Die Bildnisse der antiken Dichter, Redner und Denker*, 1943) — sculptures which could not have been created had not the artists themselves been conscious of this freedom and dignity. A great part of the present day, highly-praised "art of the free West", expresses in word and image a disgust which is perhaps pardonable — with the genus Man, often even a disgust with the "artist" himself, and it is obvious that as such, it no longer belongs to the spirit of the West, first expressed to perfection by the Hellenes. The present day West, insofar as it is represented by "famous artists", is no longer capable of grasping the totality of the world phenomenon or of the human picture. It is content to produce distorted fragments which are then regarded with astonishment by the Press as assertions about "essentials". Writers, painters, sculptors and designers depict — after their own image creatures which fall far short of the nobility of man, ranking culturally with lemurs — "semi-natures" pieced together from ligaments, sinews and bones (Goethe, *Faust*, 11, Act 5, Great courtyard of Palace), "semi-natures" whose microcephaly or even headlessness, seem to symbolise the rejection of reason, *logos, ratio* by the "artists" of the present era. As for present day lyrics, Hugo Friedrich (*Die Strurktur der modernen Lyrik*, 1961) has made a most penetrating anaylsis of them from Baudelaire to the present day and delineates a downward trend in lyricism which reflects the decline of the West, even though he does not attempt to evaluate the artistic level of modern lyricism or discuss the question whether it may in fact still be regarded as Western.

The decline of human dignity and freedom through socialism, which would demand as much state power as possible was also feared by Friedrich Nietzsche, who, like Jefferson and Wilhelm von Humboldt, recommended as little of the State as possible, and finally called the state the coldest of all cold monsters. (*Also Sprach Zarathustra: Von neuen Götzen.*) Today such an opinion would incur disciplinary action against its author — not only in eastern European states. Socialism, according to Nietzsche (*Taschenausgabe*, Bd. III, pp 350-351), coveted "a fullness of state power such as only despotism had enjoyed indeed it surpassed all the past because it strove for the formal annihilation of the individual." From a World State or a World Republic, which today is regarded by "progressive" believers as the desired goal of humanity Nietzsche expected nothing other than the final disappearance of all remnants of freedom and human dignity: "Once the earth is brought under all-embracing economic control, then mankind will find it has been reduced to machinery in its service, as a monstrous clockwork system of ever smaller, more finely adjusted wheels." (*Nietzches gesammelte Werke*, Musarionausgabe, B. XIX, 1962, p266; cf. also Charles Andler: *Nietzsche, Sa Vie et sa Pensée*, Vol. III, 1958, pp 201 *et seq.*).

The decline of freedom and human dignity under socialism was also foretold by Gustave Le Bon in his books *Psychologie des Foules* (1895) and *Les Lois psychologiques de l'évolution des Peuples* (1894). Le Bon was afraid that the masses would readily accept every subjection under strong-willed leaders, and dissolve the age-old cultures of Europe, and that in their delusion that freedom and equality could be achieved by ever-increasing legislation, they would legally whittle it away, especially as they regarded freedom as an external lack of restraint. From Caesarism, the despotism of leaders, the masses expected not so much freedom which they were not really striving after as equal subjection for all. The Socialism of our time (1895) would have the effect of state absolutism, especially as the socialism of the masses would appear as a new religion and would compel uniformity. Later the state would become almighty God. The race soul of the peoples represents their cultural condition; the mass soul of the population represents a condition of barbarism and of decline.

Theobald Ziegler, Professor of Philosophy at the University of Strasburg, stated in his work *Die Soziale Frage* (1891) a study of the socialist ideas of his time, that the equal subjection of everyone under state patronage, was a predominantly German tendency. Ernst Troeltsch, Professor of Philosophy at the University of Berlin (*Das 19 Jahrhundert*, Gesammelte Schriften, IV, Bd., p 640) wrote in 1925, that "the pressure of universal state power weighed ever-increasingly on the people". This was and is without doubt also true for those peoples who live in democracies, for, as Eduard Schwartz, the historian (*Charakterköpfe der Antike*, 1943) has stated, the civic courage of personal opinion, the courage of independent judgment, was neither a self-evident nor a superfluous virtue in democracies. The freedom of independently thinking men becomes more and more restricted in the era of the legally "liberated" masses, departmental orders and public opinion.

Into what lack of dignity and lack of freedom, into what abysses of official, spiritual and moral life, Socialist governments can lead a once noble and free people, is illustrated by the outstanding example of modern Sweden. Witness of this is the Swedish socialist Tage Lindbom, director of the Stockholm Archives for the History of the Working Class Movement, a most competent expert in his book *Sancho Panzas Väderkvarnar* (1963).

The abuse of the freedom of rural communities by hybrid city masses was responsible for decay in Hellas as well as in Rome. For Plato (*Theaitetos*, 172-173), freedom was the dignified independence of the noble man. In his work *The State* (*Politeia* VIII, 550, 557-558, 562-564), he criticised freedom as a slogan for city masses; an excess of such freedom would hand over the state as well as the individual to an excess of slavery. To a man of dignified freedom the guiding factor is merely truth (Plato: *Theaitetos*, 172-173) which is always simple; to the unworthy man, the guiding factor in freedom is gossip, slyness, flattery and persuasion by means of confused and false proofs.

In this way freedom vanished towards the end of the aristocratic Roman republic, with the extinction of the freeborn (*ingenui*); under the Emperors the freedom of the freedman (*liberti*), which was nothing less than self-restraint, started in the capital and spread to all the cities of the Empire, a freedom from which the last freeborn Romans could only withdraw, exchanging their earlier tradition of participating in state life for one of isolation. The wiseman — Cicero once wrote (*de legibus*, I, 61) — holds that what the masses praise so highly is worth nothing. Horace (*Carmina* I, 1, 2, 16, 39, 40), who had experienced the transition from the aristocratic republic into the Caesarism of the Emperors, favouring the masses, spoke of an evil-willed crowd (*malignum volgus*). The behaviour of the freedmen in flattering the Emperors has been described with contempt by Petronius, who originated from a family of the *nobilitas*, the official nobility, in his *Cena Trimalchionis*. In this satire one of the last freeborn Romans expresses his disgust, with the superior calm of a man who looks towards decline without hope. In the year 66, Petronius, hitherto popular at his court, was condemned to death by Nero.

The literature of the "free West" celebrated and praised by the reviewers and critics of today's newspapers, would probably be regarded by Petronius as a literature of freedmen for freedmen. In particular it is just those authors who are most praised today who promote with boring repetition nothing less than the further decomposition of the spiritual and moral values of the Indo-European. The newspaper writers praise the "freedom" of these "artists" in contrast with the "aesthetic backwardness" of isolated doubters. To be regarded as aesthetically backward is also the admonition of Horace: "Nothing small and nothing in a low manner! "

After the ending of colonial rule it must be feared that the populations of wide regions of the earth will behave as freedmen, all the more so as colonial rule has destroyed what remains of the ancient ethical and social orders of these populations; in other words, they will imitate large sections of the youth of "cultured peoples".

After every constitutional alteration and every upheaval since the middle of the nineteenth century, the peoples of the west have lost more of the freedom of the individual originally peculiar to their nature, and have had to bear instead more subjection, more of "the insolence of office" (Shakespeare, *Hamlet*, III, 1). Since this process took place gradually, the loss of the freedom which was inherent in the spirit of Indo-European yeomen, the loss of that freedom which although weakened and distorted, was still effective in the political liberalism of the nineteenth century, has proceeded unnoticed while calculating opportunists have readily learned how to exploit officialdom or have themselves obtained high appointment in government offices. As a result there has been a gradual but powerful growth of authoritarianism in both the state and political parties, and in the influence, exercised either openly or in secret of moneyed people behind them.

The poet Paul Ernst (1866-1937), in his enthralling *Jugend-*

erinnerungen (completed in 1929 and published in 1959) has described the transition of his homeland from a land of rural crafts-men to an industrial state accompanied by fearful losses in uprightness, solidarity and mutual regard and confidence between men — a transition bringing with it an increasing loss of freedom in which the younger men became more or less willingly entangled. The father of the poet was obliged even at the age of nine, to work in a mine in the Harz mountains as a "Pochjunge" with a weekly wage of 60 pfennigs. When twenty-two years old, he earned 2.40 marks per week; and from 1856, when he was in his twenty-third year, one Taler. The poet, his son, succumbed just as little as did his father to the blandishments of Marxism which appeared in his time; rather, he gave a warning of the universal subjection to which socialist states would be reduced as had John Stuart Mill and Herbert Spencer. The poet saw in Marxism a "path leading to a more terrible slavery than the world had ever known" (pp. 289-290). He expressed the view that today a man who wishes to avoid the embraces of such slavery, must so adapt his life that he must place himself as far as possible beyond contemporary society, and must remain completely isolated from contemporary influences. The solitude of the individual was rejected in Germany by mass-minded (Ochlocratic) National Socialism in favour of a Folk community of urban masses, which also revealed the end of the Indo-European era in Germany. But the person with understanding will realise, like Herbert Spencer, that the loss of the freedom of the individual is unavoidable in all industrial societies.

It is unfortunately true that amongst the peoples of the west, the number of men who prefer freedom to a high standard of living has become very small, and that men who are naturally freeborn (*eleutheros, ingenuus*) and Paul Ernst was one, suffer from increas-ing patronisation. In his *Jugenderinnerungen* (Memories of youth, p 312) Paul Ernst wrote that his father had always been a free man despite his poverty, and his mother a dignified woman, as befitted the wife of such a man.

There is a great need for men of the calibre of Paul Ernst, of the kind of human breed whose dying out is being hastened today, if the loss of freedom is to be noticed at all. Walter Muschg, Professor of Basle University, in an address on the occasion of the Schiller celebrations, entitled *Schiller: The Tragedy of Freedom* (1959), emphasised that freedom had "not only vanished under dictatorships, but also in the so-called free countries. Everywhere new power factors had formed which controlled the existence of men and had produced invisible forms of slavery, before which our liberal forefathers would have shuddered.... We are surrounded by Gessler hats, at which no one takes aim. Present-day man no longer knows what freedom is and furthermore he no longer desires it. He wishes for comfort, for an effortless enjoyment of life at the price of bureaucratic control for which he willingly pays. The will to freedom has been succeeded by the longing for domination, for release from self-determination. From this longing... arise both open and veiled forms of dictatorship."

MT Vaerting, who went to North America, a land of apparent freedom, when the National Socialist state in Germany became more and more totalitarian to the extent, finally of mistrusting even the private sphere of individuals who were incapable of mass existence — eventually came to the conclusion, which she expounded in two books,[44] that gradually all states in Europe and North America were following the example of Soviet Russia, and that they were on the road to the totalitarian mass state which can lead one way only, to a super-state under which freedom and human dignity are oppressed.

Thus she sees everywhere an increase in the power of the state which will bring about the decline of man. Such a decline effected through the increasing control of man by the State, will not be felt by the masses, who demand security, but will be completed through the further extinction of freeborn families, exactly as described and predicted by Walther Rathenau[45] in *The Tragedy of the Aryan People*, which Rathenau saw as the greatest tragedy of the whole of human history. However, this expiring race was, and is still, the race of Heraclitus and Sophocles, of Titus Lucretius Carus, of that same Cato Uticensis, who preferred death to life under the *dictator perpetuus* Julius Caesar; it was and is still the breed of Giordano

Bruno, Thomas Jefferson and Wilhelm von Humboldt, a breed which through its inherited qualities is still capable of a brave, undaunted struggle for dignity and freedom. *Selbst ist der Mann* (Rely on yourself)!

Socrates once walked round the market in Athens, looking at the quantity of goods on display, the luxury articles indicative of the high standard of living of the Athenians — who were otherwise spiritually impoverished — and he turned to his friends and said: "How many things there are, which I can do without!"

The products of the mass media of our age, which will soon be brought within reach of the remotest peoples on earth, at the cost of distorting and replacing their native cultures by the spiritually-destructive technology known as "world culture" will be renounced by the last true Indo-Europeans in just the same way as Socrates renounced the wares displayed for sale in the market place at Athens.

But to Indo-European man himself, the historic creator of cultures from Benares to Reykjavik, we may truly apply the words of Hamlet:

"We shall not look upon his like again!"

REFERENCES

1. HANS F. K. GÜNTHER
   Rassenkunde Europas, 1929.
   *Die Nordische Rasse bei den
   Indogermanen Asiens*, 1934.
   *Herkunft und Rassengeschichte der
   Germanen*, 1935.
   *Lebensgeschichte des hellenischen
   Volkes*, 1956.
   *Lebensgeschichte des römischen
   Volkes*, 1957.
   FRANZ ROLF SCHRÖDER
   *Germanentum und Alteuropa,
   Germanisch-Romanische
   Monatsschrift*, XXII, 1934, p 157ff
   KARL J. NARR
   Vorderasien, Nordafrika, Europa,
   in: Abriss der Vorgeschichte,
   1957, p. 6o ff.
   *Deutschland in vor-und
   frühgeschichtlicher Zeit*, in:
   Handbuch der Geschichte, Vol.1,
   1957, Section 1, page 41 ff.
   GIACOMO DEVOTO
   Origini Indeuropee, 1961.

2. BURKARD WILHELM LEIST
   Alt-arisches Jus gentium, 1889.
   Alt-arisches Jus civile, 1892-6.
   cf. *Gracco-italische Rechtsge-
   schichte*, 1884.

3. HANS F. K. GÜNTHER
   *Kleine Rassenkunde des deutschen
   Volkes*, 1933.
   Rassenkunde des deutschen Volkes,
   1934.
   WILHELM HAUER
   *Die vergleichende Religions-
   geschichte und das Indogermanen-
   problem*, in: Germanen und
   Indogermanen, Festschrift für
   Herman Hirt, edited by Helmut
   Amtz, first vol. 1936, p 177 ff
   *Glaubensgeschichte der
   Indogermanen*, Part 1, 1937.
   F. HERTER
   Die Götter der Griechen,
   Kriegsvorträge der Universität
   Bonn, No. 57, 1941.

   V. BASANOFF
   Les Dieux des Romains, 1942.
   WALTHER WOST
   Indogermanisches Behenntnis, 1942.
   GEORGES DUMÉZIL
   Jupiter-Mars-Quirinus, 1948.
   *Les Dieux des Indo-Européens à
   Rome*, 1954.
   Déesses latines et mythes védiques, 1956.
   *L'Ideologie tripartie des Indo-
   Européens*, 1958.
   Les Dieux des Germains, 1959.
   FRANZ ALTHEIM
   Römische Religionsgeschichte,
   1951-53.
   HELMUTH V. GLASENAPP
   Die Religionen Indiens, 1956.

4. ANDREAS HEUSLER
   Germanische Religion, in:
   Religion in Geschichte und
   Gegenwart, Vol. 11, 1928,
   Sp. 1041 ff.
   FRANZ ROLF SCHRÖDER
   *Die Germanen, Religionsgeschicht-
   liches Lesebuch*, Vol. XII, 1929.
   BERNHARD KUMMER
   Midgards Untergang, 1938.
   ANDREAS HEUSLER
   Deutsche, Literaturzeitung, Vol.
   XLIX, 1, 1928, Sp. 33 ff.
   FELIX GENZMER
   Hessische Blätter für Volkskunde, Vol.
   XXVII, 1928, p 217 ff.
   WILHELM GRÖNBECH
   Kultur und Religion der Germanen,
   1937.
   HERMANN SCHNEIDER
   Die Götter der Germanen, 1938.
   ERIK THERMAN
   Eddan och dess Ödestragik, 1938.
   MÜLLER-TRATHNIGG
   *Religionen der Griechen, Römer
   und Germanen*, 1954.
   JAN DE VRIES
   Altgermanische Religionsgeschichte,
   1956-7,

R. L. M. DEROLEZ
De Godsdienst der Germanen, 1959.

TURVILLE-PETRE
Myth and Religion of the North: The Religion of Ancient Scandinavia, 1964.

5. ANDREAS HEUSLER as 4 supra.

6. K. F. GELDNER
Die Zoroastrische Religion, Religionsgeschichtliche Lesebuch, Vol. 1, 1926.

HERMANN LOMMEL
Zarathustra und seine Lehre, Universitas, XII, 1957, p 267 ff.
Die Religion Zarathustras nach den Quellen dargestellt 1930.
Von arischer Religion, Geistige Arbeit, 1, 1934. No. 23 pp. 5-6.
Die Alten Arier: Van Art und Adel ihrer Götter, 1935

H. S. NYBERG
Die Religionen des Alten Irans, Mitteilungen der Vorderasiatisch-ägyptischen Gesellschaft, 34, vol., 1938.

GEO. WIDENGREN
Iranische Geisteswelt, 1961.

OTTO VON WESENDONK
Das Weltbild der Iraner, 1933.

7. WILHELM NESTLE
Griechische Religiostität von Homer bis Pindar un Aschylos, 1930, p 113.

8. SIEGFRIED LAUFFER
Die Antike in der Geschichtsphilosophie. Die Welt als Geschichte, XVI, Vols. III-IV, 1958, p 175 ff.

HANS F. K. GÜNTHER
Lebensgeschichte des römischen Volkes, 1957, p 307.

9. HANS F. K. GÜNTHER
Lebensgeschichte des hellenischen Volkes, 1956, pp 157, 195-96.

10. R. A. NICHOLSON
Studies in Islamic Mysticism, 1921, pp. 162, 180-181, 184.

A Literary History of the Arabs, 1930, pp 383 ff, 393-394.

EDUARD MEYER
Geschichte des Altertums, Vol. I, 11, 1909, pp 385-386.

1 1. WILHELM HAUER
Urkunden und Gestalten der Germanisch-Deutschen Glaubensgeschichte, 1940, ff.

FRITZ BURI
Gottfried Kellers Glaube, 1944.

12. WALTER F. OTTO
Die Götter Griechenlands, 1947.
Theophania: Der Geist der altgriechischen Religion, 1956.

ELLISWORTH BARNARD
Shelley's Religion, 1936.

13. AXEL OLRIK
Ragnarök, 1922.

STIG WIKANDER
Sur le fond commun Indoiranien des épopées de la Perse et de l'Inde, La Nouvelle Clio, Vol. VII, 1949-50, p 330 ff.
Germanische und Indoiranische Eschatologie, Kairos, Vol. 11,1960, pp 78-88.

GEORGES DUM@ZIL
Les Dieux des Germains, 1959, pp. 85, 92, 103.

14. HANS F. K. GÜNTHER
Platon als Hüter des Lebens, 1966.

15. WALTHER BAETKE
Arteigene Germanische Religion und Christentum, 1933, p 40.

HANNS RÜCKERT
Die Christianisierung der Germanen, 1934, p 20.

16. BODDHISATTVA ASVAGOSHA
A life of Buddha, Sacred Books of the East, Vol. XIX, 1883, verse I, 52, p 9, verse V, 1856, p. 270./

MAHAPADANA SUTTANTA
Dialogues of Buddha: *Sacred Books of the Buddhists*, Vol. III, Part 11, 1910, p 36.

LAKKHANA SUTTANTA
Same series, Vol. IV, Part III, 1921,
p 138.

17. ALBERT CARNOY
Les Indo-Européens, 1921, p 221.

18. MAX DEUTSCHBEIN
*Individuum und Kosmos in
Shakespeares Werken,* Shakespeare
Jahrbuch, Vol. LXIX, 1933, p 25
cf. also Erik Therman, *Eddan och
dess Ödestragik,* 1938.

19. WILHELM ENGEL
Die Schicksaisidee im Altertum,
Veröffentlichungen des
Indogermanischen Seminars der
Universität Erlangen, Vol. II,
1926, pp 45-70, 95-114.
JOHANNES MEWALDT
*Die tragische Weltanschauung der
hellenischen Hochkulter,
Forschungen und Fortschritte,*
No. 14, 1934, p 177 ff.
HANS NAUMANN
Germanischer Schicksalsglaube, 1934.
WALTHUR GEHL
Der Germanische Schicksalsglaube, 1939.
WALTER F. OTTO
Das Wort der Antike, 1962, p 334 ff.

20. HANS RÜCKERT
*Die Christianisienung der
Germanen,* 1934, p 20.

21. WILLIAM JAMES
The Varieties of Religious Experience,
1907, pp 78 ff, 127 ff.

22. GUSTAV NECKEL
Altgermanische Kultur, 1925, pp 32-33.
HANS F. K. GÜNTHER
*Die Nordische Rasse bei den Indo-
germanen Asiens,* 1934, pp. 26, 32,
111, 232.

23. ANDREAS HEUSLER
*Altgermanische Sittenlehre und
Lebensweisheit,* in: Hermann
Nollau, *Germanische Wiederers-
tehung,* 1926, p. 161.

24. VILHELM GRÖNBECH
Die Germanen, in: Chantepie de la
Saussaye, Lehrbuch der Religions-
geschichte, Vol. 11, 1925, p 563.
KURT LEESE
*Die Krisis und Wende des
Christlichen Geistes,* 1932, p 405 ff.

25. HANS F. K. GÜNTHER
Rassenkunde des jüdischen Volkes,
1930, p 26 ff.
L.F.CLAUSS
Rasse und Seele, 1940, p 146.

26. HANS F. K. GÜNTHER
*Kleine Rassenkunde des deutschen
Volkes,* 1934, p 236 ff.
Rassenkunde Europas, 1929, p 82 ff.

27. WILHELM HAUER
Die vergleichende Religionsgeschichte,
1936, p 101. See note 3 supra.

28. JULIUS VON NEGELEIN
*Die Weltanschauungen des indoger-
manischen Asiens,* Veröffentlichungen
des indogermanischen Seminars
der Universität Erlangen, Vol. 1,
1924, pp. 100 et seq.
Chantepie de la Saussaye, as 20,
1925, pp 18-19. See note 24 supra.

29. VILHELM GRÖNBECH
in Johannes Edvard Lehmann,
Illustrerad Religionshistoria, 1924,
pp 488-89. See note 4 supra.
BERNHARD KUMMER
See note 4 supra.

30. KURT SCHRÖTTER UND
WALTHER WÜST
Tod und Unsterblichkeit im
Weltbild Indogermanischer
Denker, 1942.
ALBERT CARNOY
Les Indo-Européens, 1921, p 228 ff.
PAUL THIEME
*Studien zur indogermanischen
Wortkunde und Religionsgeschichte,*
Berichte über die Verhandlungen
der Sächsischen Akademie der
Wissenschaften zu Leipzig,

phil-hist. Klasse, Vol. XCVIII,
No. 5, 1952, pp 35 ff, 55ff.

31. GUSTAV NECKEL
*Die Uberlieferungen vom Gotte
Balder,* 1920.
RUDOLF MUCH
Balder, Zeitschrift für Deutsches
Altertum, Vol. LXI, 1924, p 93 ff.
JOHANNES LEIPOLDT
*Sterbende und auferstehende
Götter,* 1923.

32. HANS F. K. GÜNTHER
*Die Nordische Rasse bei den Indo-
germanen Asiens,* 1934, pp 40, 120.

33. HANS F. K. GÜNTHER
Rassenkunde des jüdischen Volkes,
1930, p 68 ff.
L.F.CLAUSS
Rasse und Seele, p. 117.

34. HERMANN OLDENBERG
Die Lehre der Upanischaden, 1915,
pp 39 ff, 44 ff.
PAUL DEUSSEN
Die Philosophie der Upanischaden, 1919.

3 5. CHRISTIAN AUGUST LOBECK
Aglaophamus, Vol. 1, 1828, p 412.
HERMAN DIELS
Die Fragmente der Vorsokratiker,
Vol. 1, 1951, pp 113 ff, 129 ff, 217 ff.

36. PAUL DEUSSEN
Das System des Vedanta, 1883.
HELMUTH VON GLASENAPP
Der Stufenweg zum Göttlichen, 1948.

37. HERMANN MANDEL
*Deutscher Gottglaube von der
Deutscher Mystik bis zur Gegenwart,*
1934, pp 19 ff.
Wirklichkeitsreligion, 1933.

38. ALFRED BIESE
*Die Entwicklung des Naturgefühls
bei den Griechen und Römern,* 1882.
*Die Entwicklung des Naturgefühls im
Mittelalter und in der Neuzeit,* 1922.

OTTO KÖRNER
*Das Naturgefühl in der homerischen
Dichtung,* Das humanistische
Gymnasium, 45, 1934, p 119.
JOSEF STRZYGOWSKI
*Die Lantischaft in des nordischen
Kunst,* 1922.

39. HILDEBRECHT HOMMEL
Der Himmelsvater, Forschungen und
Fortschritte, Year 19, 1943, Sp 94 ff.
GIACOMO DEVOTO
Origini Indeurope, 1962, pp 251-52.

40. MAX SCHNEIDEWIN
Die antike Humanität, 1897.
Humanitas, Realencyklopidie der
klassischen Altertumswissen-
schaften, Supplement- Band V,
1931, Sp 282 ff.
HANS F. K. GONTHER
Humanitas, in: *Führeradel durch
Sippenpflege,* 1941, p 158 ff.

41. WILHELM NESTLE
*Griechische Religiosität vom
Zeitalter des Perikles bis auf
Aristoteles,* 1930, p 85.

42. BERTRAND RUSSELL
The Conquest of Happiness, 1953, p 113.
LUDWIG WINTER
Der Begabungsschwund in Europa,
1959.

43. CLAUDIUS FRHR. VON
SCHWERIN
*Freiheit und Gebundenheit im
Germanischen Staat,* Recht und
Staat in Geschichte und
Gegenwart, No. 90, 1933.

44. M. T. VAERTING
*Europa und Amerika: Der Entwick
lungsweg des Staates zum Überstaat,*
1951.
*Machtzuwachs des Staates –
Untergang des Menschen,* 1952.

45. HARRY GRAF KESSLER
Walther Rathenau, 1928, p 43.

For details of other titles available
from the Historical Review Press,
on revisionist history, ethnology, politics and philosophy
please send a stamped self-addressed envelope to:
PO Box 62, Uckfield, Sussex, TN22 1ZY, UK,
or visit our website at: www.ety.com/HRP

The **RACIAL ELEMENTS OF EUROPEAN HISTORY**
Professor Hans FK Günther. A study of the racial origins of the
European peoples, by one of the pioneers of racial science. This is
a translation from the second German edition by GC Wheeler. It
is profusely illustrated with 368 portraits of racial types, and 22
maps showing the distribution of racial types. Günther examines
the physical and mental characteristics of the five basic sub-races
of Europe, as well as the influence of racial strains from outside
Europe. He examines the development of the European races in
prehistory, with especial reference to the Nordic. After examining
contemporary Europe from the racial perspective, he closes with
a rousing chapter on the Nordic as an ideal, the result of an
anthropological view of history.

Pb, 280pp. ISBN: 0-906879-61-2.
Price: £10.95 including post & packing.

This book, and the titles on the following pages, are all available from
the Historical Review Press, PO Box 62, Uckfield, Sussex, TN22 1ZY, UK.

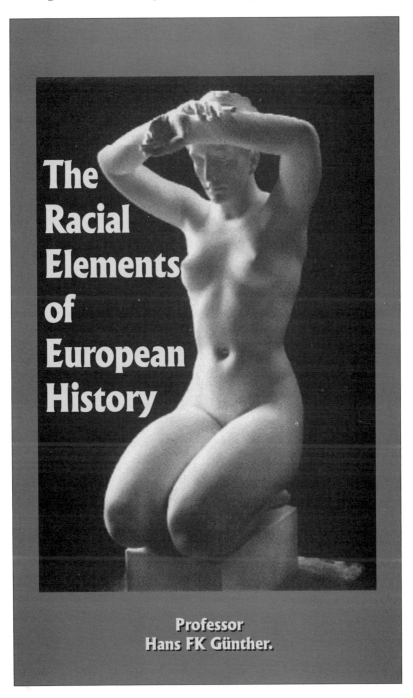

The
Racial
Elements
of
European
History

Professor
Hans FK Günther.

The ORIGINS OF CHRISTIANITY by Professor Revilo P Oliver.
Religions often succeed in being a major influence in deciding the
shape of the future. So they must be taken seriously, even by those
who find it impossible to believe in them. Revilo Oliver stood apart,
not only from liberals, but also from his 'conservative' allies who
refused to see that much of the fault for our civilisation's decline
lay in *ourselves* – in the racial and societal characteristics that have
left us nearly defenceless against an implacable, relentless and
clever enemy. He concluded that one of the major weaknesses of
our civilisation was its religion, which had been, since the latter
years of the Roman Empire, some form of Christianity. With the
objectivity of the scholar he set out, over the last decade and a
half of his life, to trace the religion to its roots in the Middle East
and to analyse the birth and mutation of its basic characters and
ideas. A stunning work from a leading classical scholar and white
patriot.

Pb 174pp. Price: £10.95 including post and packing

The Origins of Christianity

Revilo P Oliver

From the author of *The Decline of the West...*

MAN AND TECHNICS by Oswald Spengler. The follow-up to his monumental *Decline of the West*. This is a much more accessible introduction to Spenglerian philosphy of history. The fundamental premise of the book is that the world is governed by natural forces, not genteel political and religious creeds. It is the work of an astute intellect, alive to the workings of the universe; startling and refreshing it is bound to stimulate your thinking.

Paperback, 73pp. Price: £4.95 including post & packing.

Two booklets from Revilo Oliver...

REFLECTIONS ON THE CHRIST MYTH   A concise introduction to the origins of Christianity by a leading classicist, inspired by Nick Carter's book *The Christ Myth*. From the booklet: "As shown by the presence of the Magi at the birth of the non-Jewish christ, there was also an influence of the Zoroastrian cult, which by that time had assimilated both astrology and the notion that a Saviour (Saosyant) would come to deliver the world from evil... A god who could be concerned with anyone but the Chosen was utterly repugnant to the Jewish mind and a christ who could interest himself in goyim was an abomination as well as an impossibility."

Paperback booklet, 45pp. Price: £3.95 including post & packing.

THE USES OF RELIGION   A skilfull analysis of the effects of various religious movements on society, written when 'born-again' Christianity was sweeping America. From the booklet: "From the earliest history of our race to the present, religion has ... served three distinct purposes: as a political bond; as a sanction for social morality, and as a consolation for individuals."

Paperback booklet, 36pp. Price £3.00 including post & packing.

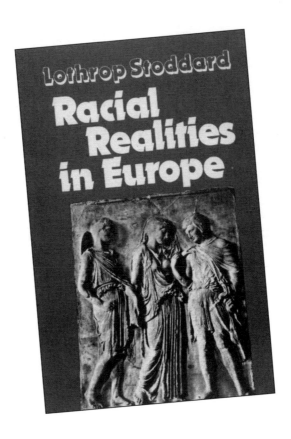

RACIAL REALITIES IN EUROPE Lothrop Stoddard   A classic study of the racial make-up of the indigenous White peoples of Europe. An authoritative study of the ethnic make-up of our people.

Pb 252pp. ISBN 0-906879-60-4
Price: £9.95 including post & packing.